D1267807

The Uses of Communication in Decision-Making

A Comparative Study of Yugoslavia and the United States

PRAEGER SPECIAL STUDIES IN INTERNATIONAL POLITICS AND GOVERNMENT

Praeger Publishers New York Washington London

Library of Congress Cataloging in Publication Data

Edelstein, Alex S
The uses of communication in decision-making.

(Praeger special studies in international politics and government)
Bibliography: p.
1. Public opinion polls. 2. Communication.
3. Decision-making. I. Title.
HM258.E3 301.16 73-15184
ISBN 0-275-28779-3

PRAEGER PUBLISHERS
111 Fourth Avenue, New York, N.Y. 10003, U.S.A.
5, Cromwell Place, London SW7 2JL, England

Published in the United States of America in 1974
by Praeger Publishers, Inc.

Printed in the United States of America

To Raymond B. Nixon,
Professor Emeritus, University of Minnesota,
Who helped me, in Vienna in 1964,
To get it all started

PREFACE

This has been an unusual experiment in cooperation in research in mass communication. It is the first and only cooperative project in this field in Yugoslavia. At almost every step there was contact between the American and Yugoslav teams.

Srdjan Sokolović spent an academic year at the University of Washington working with the author and his associate, Dr. Neil Hollander, in the conceptualization of the research. Each step in the development of the concepts and the questionnaire was communicated to Belgrade for comment. Mr. Sokolović remained in Seattle with Dr. John Mathiason and Robert Laing to carry out the Seattle field work. Dr. Hollander and I went to Belgrade to proceed with pretests and field work in Yugoslavia.

The field work in Belgrade and Ljubljana was directed by Dr. Hollander, Ms. Danojlić, and myself. Field work in Ljubljana was carried out by the Institute for Public Opinion and Mass Communication under the direction of Professor Niki Toš and his assistant, Drago Zajc.

It was my duty, as Head Researcher of a Joint Working Team, to prepare the plans for carrying out the basic goals of the research. These plans were presented each week to the working teams for review.

It is important to point out that this is the only study of the mass communication system of a Socialist country in which an American scholar has participated directly. Participation took a special form: We worked within the self-management system specified by Yugoslav policies and practices. We defined our goals as the pursuit of knowledge in a scientific and responsible manner.

According to the bilateral agreement, Milo Popović, Director of the Institute for Journalism, was nominally the project director. He exercised special initiative in making the project possible. Stevan Marajanović replaced Mr. Popović as acting director upon the latter's retirement from the Institute.

The research reflects a point of view. This perspective places great value on the need for a form of dialogue to take place between the interviewer and the respondent in which the respondent may talk about problems from his point of view. This is operationalized by a methodological approach that encourages respondents to inform us of their views rather than permitting them to respond only to our definition of the situation.

The point of view and the methodology came to the attention of our Yugoslav colleagues at a meeting in Ljubljana in 1969 on Mass Media and International Understanding. They suggested at that time that this approach could be utilized crossculturally with good effects.

We had experimented first with this approach in public opinion studies, which have, of course, their implications for mass communication. We had developed a method of defining public opinion without imposing any definition of the situation upon the respondent.

We felt a similar concern with methodologies used in some studies of mass communication. In these studies, as one example of methodological bias, respondents had been required to use the criterion of "credibility" as a means of evaluating media sources. When in our studies we permitted people to inform us freely as to how they judged the utility of their sources of information—in situations where they actually were using information—they employed criteria other than credibility. As will be reported in Chapter 20, credibility was not the most important or even a strongly relevant criterion for our respondents.

Our methodology also carried important implications for developmental studies in mass communication. Persons in these studies who had been defined as illiterate (because of lack of education, for example) were shown to have used far fewer print media than the better educated and hence more literate respondents. (Literacy also was determined by general tests of language skills and knowledge.)

From our point of view, literacy should be conceptualized only in functional terms: that is, the ability of an individual to use literacy skills with respect to a problem with which that person is concerned. It should not be a general test but a specific one. In our data, unlike the findings in other developmental studies in mass communication, the least educated members of the sample population reported that they used print media to a considerable extent to learn about problems with which they were attempting to cope.

This finding is not too difficult to explain: One tries to learn, by whatever means, about one's problems—living quarters and housing, as an example, if one is seeking a place to live. Housing was a local problem named by many of our Belgrade respondents. We ourselves had often watched crowds of people in Belgrade waiting patiently outside the newspaper plants for the evening editions that would carry classified advertisements for rooms, apartments, flats, and houses. Many of the persons who needed the housing so desperately were peasants who were illiterate by testing standards, but they learned to read a classified advertisement. They became functionally literate for this purpose. Our methodological approach permitted these peasants to talk to us about their needs and how they used newspapers—among other sources of information—to cope with those needs.

What is offered here, therefore, is more than a conventional approach to the study of communication and decision-making. We are attempting, through a fresh methodological approach, to provide new dimensions of knowledge about how people use mass communication.

I wish to express my special appreciation to Edmond Bator, First Cultural Attaché of the American Embassy in Belgrade, for his continuing support of the goals of this project.

In the United States Information Agency, Washington, D.C., special thanks must go to Raymond Benson, former Cultural Attaché in Belgrade. He and Stevan Marajanović of the Institute of Journalism first discussed this project with me.

Dr. Hollander played an important role in the development of the methodology and in the conduct of the research. Professor France Vreg, Assistant Dean of the Higher School of Political Science and Journalism in Ljubljana, was a greatly esteemed colleague there.

The School of Communications editorial secretary, Mercedes MacDonald, prepared the several reports and versions of the manuscript. I also was assisted by Rob Laing and Diane Tefft, graduate students, and Trudy Flynn, administrative assistant in the School of Communications. Masa Marajanović assisted me in secretarial duties in Belgrade. Other members of the Working Team there with whom we had the most rewarding collaboration were Jelena Stakić Danoljlić and Lilijiana Donović.

The University of Washington and the Institute for Journalism in Belgrade join in appreciation of the financial and administrative support of the National Science Foundation of the United States, the Department of Education and Cultural Affairs of the Department of State, and the Federal Agency for International Technical Cooperation of Yugoslavia, through which the project was administered in Yugoslavia as a project in technical assistance.

CONTENTS

INTRODUCTION: YUGOSLAV PERSPECTIVES

Milo Popović

The orientations and directions of this research have grown out of the need to discover the ways in which information is used by individuals and to learn of additional possibilities for its more effective use.

For each contemporary society, the uses of information are of special interest and have specific implications for decision-making on both the individual and the group level. For Yugoslavs considering a self-management structure, the processes of individual decision-making and of communication have certain special applications.

Mass communication and interpersonal communication in a self-management society have as their first objective the need to give individuals as complete and objective a picture of situations, problems, and their accompanying conditions as is possible. In this way the people may gain a complete understanding of the environment in which they live and work, may directly and through collective means decide about their special and general interests, and may express themselves as independent personalities.

The value of each individual should be demonstrated by his decision-making processes and the factors he takes into account. Decision-making in a self-management society is not simply a matter of the individual solving his own psychological or ideological problems independent of others; instead, it is a process of taking into consideration those personal and general interests on which every self-management decision should rest.

Making decisions requires information that is current and universal from a variety of sources. Being informed reflects the

---

Milo Popović is former Director of the Institut za Novinarstvo (Institute for Journalism), Belgrade, Yugoslavia.

individual's learning and conscience about social problems and is essential for each individual's affirmation as a social being and for decision-making at the collective level.

The Institute for Journalism in Belgrade, Yugoslavia, has been interested in the study of how much information and what kinds of information truly realize their place in social self-managing functions. It has also wished to learn about the physical and cognitive barriers to the diffusion of information that prevent the full utilization of information in decision-making. These interests motivated the Institute for Journalism to develop with the School of Communications, University of Washington, capabilities in theoretical and methodological approaches, especially the studies of communication and decision-making explicated by those who joined us in the present work.

Our project, entitled "The Uses of Communication in Decision-Making," which our institution undertook to realize in collaboration with the University of Washington, was focused upon an inquiry into how individuals in Seattle and in two cities in Yugoslavia—Belgrade and Ljubljana—use interpersonal and mass communication to understand the nature of social problems and to decide, if possible, what should be done about them.

We were not interested in the nature of the problems themselves, for these would vary from time to time and from one culture and urban setting to another. Rather, we were concerned with the ways in which individuals learned about problems and engaged in communication about them. This is a study of what is known about urban and world problems and the sources of that knowledge. It is not research about the problems themselves.

The research reported in this book is crosscultural in the best sense. It suggests ways in which individuals in different cultures are similar as well as different in their communication about problems. By learning about common behavior as well as differences, we became alert to more positive potentialities for communication across cultures.

The concepts in this book were an extension of earlier work in studies of communication and decision-making by Dr. Edelstein in cooperation with Dr. Neil Hollander, his associate. The reports of these first researches at a conference in Ljubljana first called our attention to the potentialities of the theory and methodology.

The research focus is situational rather than general. We did not ask about the sources of learning and other communication behavior related to general social problems but rather to specific social problems. We developed a questionnaire that gives attention first to problems of the local community and then to problems of the world community. The methodology permitted us to gain knowledge from the respondent about each kind of problem.

Our next step was to specify the ways in which the individuals and collectivities defined the nature of each problem. We borrowed again from the language of the original work by referring to these as "discrimination processes." These discrimination processes were noted in relation to both problems and possible solutions.

The media were a major focus of our work. We were interested in media as sources of information and advice, and in how media and interpersonal communication were evaluated. The individuals interviewed were described by their educational qualifications, age, sex, profession, and other social characteristics. We were interested in how the social progress of the individual and the collectivity might be related to the uses and functions of communication.

Here in Yugoslavia there are specific practical implications for the communicator in the preparation of media content. He can act as a creator and transmitter of information that will provide his audiences with the information they need as a basis for individual and collective decision-making. Or the media might choose to transmit information about problems and their solutions that is of specific concern to those in ultimate positions of decision-making.

The Institute for Journalism is concerned with the manner and the extent to which the mass media—and implicitly, the journalist—clearly recognize and deal comprehensively and creatively with the problems faced by the individual and the collectivity. We share with the journalist the desire to have the media act as sources of relevant information about a society's problems rather than merely reflecting the problems that most easily come to attention.

Our model fits the needs of communicators who focus upon the orientational situation of their audiences and seek to direct information toward the needs of individuals. This approach has the purpose of focusing observations so as to give us insight into the state and structure of the audience's knowledge. It explores connections with many variables, including those described as cognitive as well as such social factors as age, education, income capability, sex, and mobility within and contributions to the society.

Our findings should have specific practical implications for the communicator in his preparation and placement of media content. Communicators can act more responsibly by providing information that is of significance to the audience as well as to those responsible for carrying out public policies.

In this research we were not engaged in historical or ideological approaches. We limited ourselves to the theoretical and empirical aspects we defined. The greater values and meanings of the research are discussed in the context of a situation appropriate to the culture of which the data is a residual part.

We recognize the limitations of our inquiry. There are many other situations that might be studied, employing our methodological approach, when both individuals and collectivities face new problems.

This research explores only a particular dimension of how people learn about local and world problems and their ability to make decisions about them. While from our point of view the human being is rooted in a natural historical reality, this may vary, given his relations with social situations or with other people.

The larger context for our research must be the world surrounding men and women and influencing their behavior; that is, the environment in which they live and work, in which the social institutions and social norms determine their behavior.

PART I

CONCEPTUALIZATION OF THE RESEARCH

CHAPTER

1

AN ALTERNATE APPROACH TO CONCEPTUALIZATION AND METHODOLOGY

This approach to the study of mass communication differs from conventional approaches in a number of ways.

We did not test our respondents to see how much they knew about local and world problems that we specified. We did not ask everyone about pollution, or about transportation, or housing, or war or peace. We asked each respondent to talk about any problem that was important to him or her, personally, at that time.

Nor did we suggest to respondents possible sources of information about those problems. We did not ask, "Have you learned about . . . from newspapers, magazines, television, radio, or friends?" We asked respondents to tell us how they learned about their problems without ourselves suggesting problems or sources to them.

We did not ask respondents if they agreed with any given solutions for those problems. Rather, we asked if the respondent, personally, had decided what should be done. If the respondent replied affirmatively, we then asked _if_ he or she was aware of other solutions that had been proposed. We did not, ourselves spell out what those solutions might be.

From our earlier research we learned that many individuals have little or no knowledge about certain problems, they may or may not be aware of certain sources of information, they may or may not be trying to solve that problem, and they may or may not be aware of solutions proposed by others.

Hence, supplying such information to them is intrusive. We also concluded that it was necessary to ask respondents about problems that were important to them, personally, and that were as specific and situational as possible. We did not want them to play the role of observers of other persons, nor did we wish to have their own generalized nonsituational responses.

We therefore did not ask respondents about attitudes toward war and peace in general but about their knowledge and actions with respect to a particular war or peace event. We reasoned that respondents could better describe their knowledge and beliefs about a particular problem than about a general class of problems.

Theories about the uses of mass communication have traditionally been inferred primarily from attitudinal studies. Comparatively little data has been generated from situational studies. By looking at situations, we felt we could begin to build mass communication theory that was based more upon behavior than upon attitudes.

By looking at behavior in a situation, we could observe new variables. Most of these would be associated with cognitive behavior. For example:

1. Wherever individuals were able to state that important problems existed, problem awareness could be defined as a variable.
2. When respondents described the problem, distinguishing it from other problems, this implied problem definition as a variable.
3. Where respondents compared one problem to another on some common basis, pertinence or problem comparison were variables.
4. When individuals were able to decide what should be done to solve a problem, this could be defined as decision-making.
5. When respondents were able to name additional solutions that had been suggested by others, this suggested solution orientation.

This identification of parameters of cognitive behavior permitted comparisons of individuals in relation to the uses of mass communication. Individuals could be compared not merely by age, sex, education, income, or other roles but in terms of these cognitive behaviors as well.

We employed several terms to describe cognitive behavior. The two most important terms were objects and attributes.

Objects, as we used the term, referred to problems that were being described or evaluated. Any problem—whether transportation, housing, or war or peace—was an object. We used the term object rather than problem because object has a more universal meaning in the social sciences.

Attributes were the means used to describe or evaluate an object. In this case, reasons for a problem being important took on the nature of attributes. We adopted the term attribute because, as is the case with objects, it has a more universal meaning in the social sciences.

In keeping with this conceptualization, we may talk about solutions to problems also as objects, and about reasons for adopting or rejecting a solution as attributes of the solutions.

We were interested in a number of different kinds of attributes. One kind of attribute was a statement comparing one object to another. A person might use an attribute such as cost, difficulty, or time as a basis for comparing one problem with another; for example, "A" is more costly (attribute) than "B". Another attribute style was to distinguish A from B; for example, A was costly while B required too much time—each had a quality not possessed by the other. A third attribute style was to use oneself as the attribute: The person simply said that the problem was important because it was important to him, personally.

We wished to learn if users of different attribute styles used and evaluated media differently. If attributes that compared objects were more cognitively complex than attributes that made objects "distinctive," we might expect more varied media use and evaluation to be associated with "comparison" rather than "distinguishing" attributes. And both might be higher-order attributes than attributes that merely described the importance of a problem by saying, "It is important because it is important to me, personally."

One important question was whether individuals in different cultures used the same kinds of attribute styles in describing focal objects. Our pretests in Finland and Yugoslavia indicated that these attribute styles were in fact used and were "equivalent" in this sense. The question for crosscultural research became one of the extent to which each type of attribute was used. We could ask which kinds of social groups in each culture were most likely to use each style, and the effectiveness of decision-making related to each style.

There was a corollary need for equivalence of objects. We approached the problem of "object equivalence" as follows: Just because problems had similar names, they need not be similar across cultures; that is, objects with similar names might have different attributes. Thus we would be inviting only semantic confusion if we assumed that same-named objects were equivalent in meaning. We therefore rejected the idea of comparing same-named objects.

An alternative was to ignore the names, or even the attributes of objects, and allow individuals to discuss any object. The respondent could suggest the object to be discussed. Equivalence would be achieved by asking all respondents to discuss the objects most important to them, personally. (In such a case, we should ask the individual "Why?" and obtain an attribute for why this problem was important, personally, to the individual; that is, we could obtain an attribute for the attribute.) Equivalence of objects would be in terms of the importance of each object to the respondent. If each person described his or her most important object, e.g., problem, comparisons on the basis of this equivalence should be meaningful.

The individuals who were orienting themselves to these objects also could be said to be equivalent with respect to socially identifying characteristics such as age, sex, education, and income. We would combine or control social characteristics so as to provide the greatest possible degree of equivalence across social groupings in our three cultures.

Our ultimate research design for crosscultural analysis could then be viewed schematically as follows:

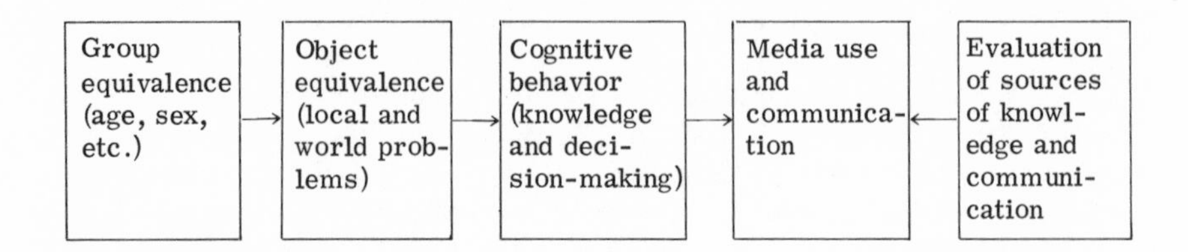

Commonalities in findings could be said to be a function of the equivalencies that were specified; differences could be said to be due to cultural factors. We would speculate as to the impact of some cultural differences, since all these differences could not be specified. (We have, however, attempted to specify some relevant cultural parameters in Chapter 4.)

In pretesting the questionnaire in a seminar at the University of Tampere in Finland, we learned that the Finns had several meanings for the word "problem." One meaning was "irresolvable." Since we were to ask respondents about "proposed solutions" to problems, it was evident that we should not use a word for "problem" that meant "irresolvable problem." Examining the semantic properties of "problem" and "most important problem" in our three focal cultures—Belgrade, Ljubljana, and Seattle—we found them to have common meanings, i.e., resolvable.

In our approach we nonetheless faced related problems:

1. The possibility that one "most important" problem might be more or less important than another "most important" problem. This could be the product of some unusual event.

We encountered such a difficulty in Seattle with respect to a local problem: Seattle was hard hit at the time of our interviewing by the local problem of unemployment. (We conducted interviewing in two waves to minimize the effect.) The question became one of how much behavior was focused upon this unusual problem; did this problem focus so much behavior at a particular time as to make comparisons with other problems—in that culture and in other cultures—untenable? We also faced this question with respect to the world problem that concerned our Seattle sample in the war in Vietnam. This question, we concluded, could be answered empirically. As we will indicate, there were some effects.

2. The possibility that it would be difficult for the respondent to focus upon a single most important problem. This difficulty was

occasionally expressed by respondents; the implication was that they were prepared to discuss any of several problems they had named. Where individuals did not identify a "most important" problem, the interviewer discussed with the respondent the first "important problem" the respondent had mentioned. (This met our test of a situationally located object in time and space. But it did not directly meet the problem of specification of a "most important" problem.)

3. We also were interested in the number of problems an individual could name at a particular time and the extent to which he could describe them. The more focal objects in one's cognitive field, the broader the knowledge and problem orientation. Presumably, varying breadths of problem orientation would produce different uses and evaluation of communication and mass communication.

4. We also thought it would be worthwhile to compare those who had the most knowledge about problems with those who had the least knowledge. How useful was knowledge in itself? This would be relevant knowledge; that is, attributes that described the focal objects.

A filter question first asked, "Which of these problems that you have mentioned is the most important to you, personally?"

Given the response, we then asked, "Why is this problem more important than the others you have mentioned?"

The number of reasons a respondent gave for the importance of the problem was a quantitative measure of knowledge. The nature of the attributes—whether comparison, distinguishing, or use of self as an attribute—provided a qualitative measure of knowledge.

5. There also could be knowledge about solutions. These, too, were objects. A question therefore asked, "Now let me ask you about another aspect of the problem. What should be done to solve the problem?"

This was followed by the question, "What other solutions have been proposed?"

The number of solutions should be a significant indication of the individual's orientation to decision-making. Awareness of other proposed solutions was presumptive of a broader context for decision-making.

6. As an inevitable question, we were interested in determining which of these cognitive variables contributed—and contributed most—to an understanding of communication behaviors. Was the number of objects in his cognitive field related to the uses and evaluation of communication? To the number of attributes for those focal objects? To the nature of the attributes? To the number of solutions? Which of these contributed, and how much, to an explanation of the uses and evaluation of interpersonal and mass communication?

7. Finally, in this analysis of groups, we wished to consider an alternative question: How well were the activities of individuals

represented by this aggregate analysis? To explain: Was there only an "average" man, woman, youth, laborer, intellectual, problem-definer, or decision-maker? Did all members of these "groups" share sources of knowledge and employ similar modes of evaluation for the utility of these sources? Obviously not. Our reports of behavior represented only "constructed collectivities" and patterns of behavior that only loosely defined individual behaviors.

To exploit the potential of our methodology for describing the behavior of individuals, we summarized profiles of respondents selected at random. These profiles suggest the validity of the social groupings we formulated. And they hint, as well, at the range of individual differences that are submerged in any collectivity.

Overall, our research represents an effort to identify capacities for problem definition and decision-making in society at a particular time in relation to the uses and evaluation of communication. As a development concept, a number of carefully planned, problem-oriented studies of this kind should reflect a society's progress in giving attention to different problems and solutions. Additional studies of this type would permit us to relate the uses of communication and mass communication to individual decision-making in a more direct and functional way than has been presented in alternate approaches.

CHAPTER

2

THE DERIVATION OF THE METHODOLOGY

Our methodology was designed to permit easy quantitative as well as qualitative analysis and to overcome problems created by conventional methods of questionnaire construction that have made it difficult to observe individuals in their own contexts.

Respondents in conventional field surveys usually are permitted to judge only those problems that have been presented to them. They are not permitted to propose the problems themselves. Respondents also are required by conventional methodologies to judge problems by criteria that may not be familiar to them.

As stated by the author (1974) and in papers in collaboration with Hollander (1968, 1970): Problems that social scientists present to respondents are not always familiar to respondents. The criterion for judging the problem also may not be familiar to the respondent. Often that criterion, if familiar, might not be the basis upon which the respondent would make his personal decision.

Pretest procedures are often used to cope with these errors. Open-ended questions are designed to elicit the important problems and the means used for judging them. Where problems and criteria for judging them are widely known, the social scientist is on safe ground. But where problems are only emerging (as is often the case) and where the means for evaluating these problems are not universally understood, it is hazardous to state them in a singular context.

Methodologists have recognized the problems of validity that occur when elements of content are imposed upon respondents. Under such circumstances, the social scientist may be observing primarily behavior that he has created by the content of his questions.

Any methodology, of course, is intrusive. In a desire to avoid errors of imposition of content, we sought to articulate a methodology that was relatively content free. This took the form of questions that were open-ended in form but systematic in order and structure.

By introducing a systematic order of questions, we posed the possibility of systematic error. However, we proceeded on the assumption that individuals do move from one point to another in consideration of a problem. In short, there must be order and system. One sequence, or order, would be problem definition, followed by an effort to cope with the problem. We assumed that all individuals define problems and cope with problems in some way, even if they decide not to cope.

We concluded that, in terms of order, we should ask individuals first to describe the nature of their problem and then to describe how they were coping with it. The alternative was to assume that individuals had solutions that were seeking problems. While some behavior appeared to operate in this way, it was obvious that to adapt a solution to a problem one also had to decide if the solution fitted the problem. Thus in any case, problem identification was essential.

VALIDATION BY QUESTIONNAIRE

Empirical evidence of the appropriateness of the approach was, of course, sought. This was provided by means of questionnaires that were administered to both interviewers and respondents.

Respondents were asked one open-ended question in their personal interview. A second, mailed questionnaire, was sent to 10 percent of the sample of respondents in Belgrade and in Ljubljana. (We had undertaken similar methodological studies earlier in Seattle, so we did not repeat this procedure.)

We looked for comments not only as to the phrasing of questions but also as to possible restrictions upon what the individual was able to report. Did the questions require the respondent to think in ways that he did not customarily think, or prevent him from describing ways in which he did think? If the respondent said "yes" to the question designed to elicit any such reports, the interviewer was instructed to write down whatever was said in amplification of the response.

Let us look first at the evaluations given to us by our interviewers: On a seven-point scale of very satisfactory to very unsatisfactory, only 6 percent of the Belgrade interviewers were on the negative part of the scale. Some 22 percent were neutral, while 72 percent rated the questionnaire as satisfactory. This broke down into 31 percent satisfactory, 28 percent very satisfactory, and 13 percent the most satisfactory system possible.

Almost half of the interviewers said that the method of interviewing was more interesting than any other kind of interviewing they had ever undertaken, and only 3 percent said it was less interesting. Of the interviewers with previous paid experience, 75 percent said the system was more interesting than any other method they had utilized.

Let us turn now to evaluations by our respondents. Some 200 postcards were mailed to respondents in Belgrade. They showed that interviews had been completed with 97.6 percent of the individuals who had been enumerated (a total of 127 cards were returned). There were only 2 percent unrecorded respondent substitutions. Responding to the question, "Were you satisfied with the interview?" one hundred percent responded "yes," a remarkable figure. (In the semantics of this response, we feel the meaning should be interpreted as follows: Nothing occurred to evoke a criticism of the conduct of the interview.)

Some 23 percent of the respondents commented on the interviews. Of the total sample, 11 percent complained about such problems as (1) too limited space in which to record their feelings, (2) too much space, (3) too much repetition of questions—actually, the question "probes," (4) not enough questions, (5) too many questions, or (6) questions of the wrong kind. Distributed among all of these comments, this represented a small proportion in each category.

Another 2 percent of the total sample wanted more time to think about local or world problems before they were interviewed about them, indicating that the respondents felt some limited demands for information they did not have. Interestingly, 9 percent wanted to add even more information about local and world problems and propose additional solutions for them. Some respondents expressed the hope that the interviews would have some effect upon getting problems solved.

A similar question, "Have you any remarks on our questionnaire?" was asked at the time of the interview, with highly similar results. We compared the responses of those who had been interviewed in person and by card. Of the 127 who also replied by card, two-thirds gave highly consistent responses on the two occasions.

Of those who changed their views in the later, mailed card, most of the changes were shifts to a more positive attitude. These respondents, upon reflection, concluded that the interview (1) had been more interesting, or (2) should have been done earlier, or (3) could be made even broader to capture even more opinions. Far fewer were critical in the sense that the questionnaire had been too extensive or repetitive.

Some 28 percent in Ljubljana, as compared to 23 percent in Belgrade, commented on the questionnaire. The pattern of responses within this group was almost identical to that observed in Belgrade, both with respect to the nature of comments and the favorable change from the earlier personal interview to the mailed questionnaire card. In Ljubljana, 160 cards were sent out and 147 cards were returned. Of these, 99 percent of the respondents said they were "satisfied" with the interview.

A summary of the replies of respondents and interviewers to all questionnaires can be grouped into four categories:

1. No remarks: An absence of remarks, given an opportunity to comment, supported an inference of a lack of intrusiveness (among other possible inferences).

2. Specific criticism of the questionnaire: Some respondents described the questionnaire as "repetitious." In our judgment, the comment referred as much to questions that elicited the same response as to the structure of questions demanding or only permitting the same response. To explain: We had focused upon two objects: a local problem and a world problem. The questions about these focal objects were similarly phrased but they focused on different objects—that is, a local problem and then a world problem. We speculated that some respondents had only one response to be elicited with respect to either object; hence, they felt the questions were repetitive.

There were a few references to "forcing the individual to think in a certain way" or, as the corollary, to "not permitting him to think in ways he preferred." But these were very infrequent. In fact, they were not numerous enough to tabulate.

3. Specific praise for the questionnaire: Respondents praised the questionnaire for essentially one reason—the results sharpened their awareness of problems and helped them to articulate them in their own minds. The respondents apparently found it helpful to discuss the problem. However, this appears to be only a qualified argument for the validity of the approach. Perceived helpfulness might either reflect a valid articulation of what people actually thought or, contrarily, represent the guiding of thought. In that sense, our methodology would be intrusive.

4. Liking or disliking the questionnaire without specification: It was difficult to interpret these responses in terms of structural bias. However, it is worth noting that these responses were distributed much more in favor of than against the questionnaire.

There was a high degree of agreement between respondents and interviewers; interviewers, however, were even more positive than respondents. Also, when we compared the responses of the most experienced interviewers with those of the least experienced interviewers, the more experienced demonstrated greater favorability.

VALIDATION BY ANALYSIS OF DATA

A second way of testing the validity of our observational approach was to examine the nature of the data. We asked two kinds of questions:

1. Were respondents equally able to respond to the questionnaire? We wanted to be certain that there were no inhibiting effects upon the old, the young, the educated, the uneducated, the urban cosmopolite, or the peasant recently moved into the city. As will be

seen, this test appeared to be met by the data. Compared to other so-called "development" research, our uneducated, our peasant, and other groupings were far more involved than conventionally derived.

2. Was this behavior related in expected ways to other behavior? As examples, we would expect that the educated would be more informed about problems than the uneducated, and would be more able to provide solutions for the problems. Actually, we expected less striking differences between groups because our questionnaire methodology permitted all respondents to discuss problems of importance to them, personally. This expectation was validated by our data.

A related and critical question with respect to the validity of the methodology was the amount of behavior that could be produced by an open-ended questionnaire. Obviously, no methodology could elicit all the behavior in which a respondent was engaged and upon which he was able to report. But we required an adequate and representative sampling of behavior.

A few respondents did not, on first questioning, report all of the behavior they were able to give. As an example, when respondents were shown a list of sources of information—after having been questioned without being shown a list—some respondents recalled, "Oh, yes. I also learned about that problem from 'radio,' 'television,' 'in a meeting . . .'"

We instructed our interviewers to give the respondent "credit" for all media behavior that was claimed. We estimated that 15 percent of the respondents added one or more sources when they saw lists of media sources. An alternative would have been to give the respondents the list of sources at the beginning. However, we concluded that this would be too suggestive at that point. The fact that we later were able to demonstrate variance in the reporting of sources of information, and that this data was internally consistent with other data, testifies to the validity of this approach.

USE OF THE PROBE

An integral part of the methodology was the concept of the probe. The purpose of the probe was to assure that a sufficient sample of behavior was obtained so as to permit both the range of individual behavior and an adequate amount of behavior to emerge.

In earlier research we found that one probe produced the optimum additional bit of behavior that was required in most cases. Two probes produced more information than one probe, but the increment was not large enough to justify the additional demand on the respondent. Nor was that increment required for purposes of data analysis.

We worked out coding procedures that in many cases required us to code only whether or not the person responded; the questionnaire was in the sense open-ended in form but closed-ended in structure.

ADMINISTRATION OF THE QUESTIONNAIRE

The questionnaire took less than 30 minutes, on the average, to administer in an interpersonal, home setting. It did not ask the individual to evaluate his problems with someone else's criteria or someone else's problems with his own criteria. Or someone else's problems with someone else's criteria. Thus the time of the respondent was conserved.

The cost of administration was less than by using a conventional approach.

Also, the questionnaire was less biased with respect to the less educated because it did not demand reading skills.

Special training of interviewers was necessary, not because of the complexity of the instrument but because of the "set" of interviewers who were accustomed to conventional administration of preformulated statements. We found a natural tendency for interviewers to formulate or reformulate interviewee responses. We therefore worked out a systematic way of preventing and correcting such interviewer bias. Our quality control centered upon questions that demanded the most activity on the part of the interviewer.

EVALUATION OF METHODOLOGY

In summary, our approach tended to reduce very appreciably the imposition upon respondents of problem error and criterion error as well as conclusions that they might not themselves propose. While it introduced an element of structural bias (forcing people to "think" in a certain way), the bias did not appear to be dysfunctional in any way for any significant number of respondents.

The methodology permitted the respondent freedom to define his own context and to express himself freely within it. Internal and external indicators of validity were present.

It also produced an adequate sample of behavior of the respondent. Probes assured the amount of behavior necessary to meet measurement requirements.

There was a high degree of concordance between respondents and interviewers in their evaluation of the methodology. It obtained the most approval from the most experienced interviewers.

Finally the methodology was administratively feasible. Interviewer training, coding, and cost were manageable.

CHAPTER 3
SAMPLING DESIGN

It was impossible to find sampling criteria that could be applied equally to the three cities. We therefore decided to sample from the populations in what were regarded as the urban settings.

In Yugoslavia, the parameters were established according to what the Yugoslav Bureau of Census has termed the "Narrower Statistical Area" of the city. For Belgrade, this included all the city's administrative districts but not the surrounding villages. The large satellite cities, Zemun and Novi Belgrade, were included in this definition. In Ljubljana, the central area and contiguous new housing areas were incorporated.

In Seattle, we used what is commonly referred to as the "metropolitan area"—the core city and the suburbs directly dependent upon the urban center.

From each of these three cities we drew a multistage random sample of the adult population—those individuals 18 years old and older. Our sample mixes were 800 for Ljubljana, 1,000 for Belgrade, and 700 for Seattle.

Our samples in both Belgrade and Ljubljana were drawn from the voting lists that are maintained by all administrative districts within the city. These lists contained, in addition to the name and address of each voter, the sex, date of birth, and parents' names. These lists were the populations from which we drew random samples.

The interviewing was conducted in Belgrade from October 13 to November 12, 1970. Some 93 percent of the interviews were completed within the first two weeks of interviewing. Interviewing in Ljubljana began in January and was completed within a three-week period. Interviewing in Seattle was begun in late November, and a second wave of interviewing was conducted in February.

Readers might be especially interested in our sampling plan in Yugoslavia because of its special nature. Interviews in Belgrade and

Ljubljana were divided proportionally among opština (districts). Each opština was divided into a number of izborna mesta (neighborhoods), which are irregular in size (typically, they varied between 300 and 1,000 voters). In order to have a basis from which to draw a clustered sample, we created new sampling units within each opština. We redivided the opština into units of 1,000, following the pattern of contiguous izborna mesta within areas of reasonable size. This was intended to reduce travel and callback time.

Approximately 10 interviews were taken from each of the sampling units of 1,000 selected. Within a geographic area probably no larger than three izborna mesta, the interviewer would conduct ten interviews.

To illustrate: The opština of Cukarica has 45,830 voters who are located in 48 izborna mestas. Proportionally, on the basis of 1,000 interviews in the city of Belgrade, 82 interviews should be conducted in the opština. Dividing the opština into units of 1,000, there were 46 sampling units. Since we wished to conduct 10 interviews within each sampling unit, we needed only 8 units to fill our quota of 82. (The two remaining interviews were randomly distributed among eight sampling units. If the remaining number was greater than five, another sampling unit was defined.) These 8 units were selected on the basis of 10 acceptable sequential numbers from a table of random numbers. For the selection of the 10 individuals within each sampling unit, again the table of random numbers was used; that is, we selected 10 individuals from the 1,000 on the basis of 10 acceptable sequential three-digit random numbers.

From each of the sampling units selected, an additional sample of 10 individuals was chosen, by the same method outlined above. This constituted the reserve list. The interviewer was given 5 reserve names and addresses, and an additional 5 were retained by the interviewer supervisor.

In Seattle, a multistage sampling system was used. The metropolitan area was gridded into equally sized population districts and numbered consecutively. A random sample then was drawn of these units. All blocks then were enumerated and a random sample of blocks was chosen.

A number of sampling units was determined for each block to meet the criterion number of respondents. Interviewers were assigned blocks and given instructions as to sampling intervals to be observed and the sex of the respondent to be interviewed. Interviewers were trained in part by a joint American-Yugoslav team that had also participated in the Yugoslav phase of the study.

No reserve lists were given to interviewers in Seattle. Rather, they were required to request substitutions. Because of a higher rate of refusals than in Yugoslavia, a higher proportion of substitutions was required.

Since cities, as such, are politically defined rather than socially integrated, we were less concerned with an accurate representation of the city than with a lack of bias in selection and with obtaining an adequate sample of the kinds of behaviors we sought to examine. Nonetheless, the sample met the criteria that are commonly set and, more important, the relevant behaviors that we sought to observe.

CHAPTER

4

THE CULTURAL AND MEDIA CONTEXTS

Mass communication, like any expressive form, is both a vehicle of culture and itself a form of culture. In our present research, however, we looked at mass communication only as a vehicle of culture rather than as a form of culture. Therefore, our questions about communication and mass communication were intended to observe what cultural values were reflected in media use and evaluation.

We did not pose these questions as explicitly stated hypotheses based upon culturally derived hypotheses. Rather, we took the more simplistic view that similarities that were transmitted would reflect common underlying cultural experiences in our three cultures. The differences would reflect divergencies in past experience or in immediately relevant contingencies.

The most obvious example of common situational parameters that produced similar communications behaviors across cultures would be the urban context itself. Such factors as place and kind of work, transportation, housing, and social life would have such similarities across cultures that they would transcend cultural differences. We assumed that—given the impelling similarities across urban cultures—any differences observed in communication and decision-making might be thought of as elements of culture that had survived the impact of urbanization. Or we might attribute differences to the varying availability and character of communication in the three urban settings.

THE CULTURAL CONTEXT

Substantial differences in cultural inheritance exist in our two Yugoslav cities. They are so substantial, in one sense, that they tend to make remarkable the impact of present urban experience as well as the integrating forces that are at work in the national context.

The most obvious precursor conditions and differences involve the distinctive ethnic character of the two cities. Belgrade is distinctively Serbian in its ethnic character, so much so (more than 95 percent) that we did not find it useful, based upon a pretest, to ask for nationalities in our final questionnaire. The same was true with respect to Ljubljana, which is overwhelmingly Slovenian, with only small Austrian, Italian, and Croatian presence.

While Yugoslavia has a significant proportion of what it terms "nationalities," these were not present in our two communities. These in some cases large minorities are centered primarily in small towns, although they make up the majority in the two autonomous provinces of Vojvodina and Kosovo (part of the Socialist Federated Republic of Serbia).*

Serbia was under the control of the Turks from the fourteenth century to the first half of the nineteenth century. Slovenia (as well as Croatia, Bosnia, and Vojvodina) was incorporated in the Austro-Hungarian monarchy. In the Middle Ages, however, these were independent states with high standards of culture and civilization.

Serbia reached the apex of power and prosperity under the reign of Emperor Dusan in the fourteenth century. Yugoslavia was affected by the classical influences of Greece and Rome, the Byzantine empire, and later Central Europe. While Serbia and Slovenia felt different influences, the Balkan Peninsula is on the crossroads between Central Europe and the Near East, and since time immemorial it has been a point of intersection of cultural and political influence.

Some of the cultural differences that exist today among the Yugoslav nationalities are a product of different levels of economic development. A report by Majstorović for UNESCO (1969) noted that the geographical and cultural map of the country by the end of World War II was marked by formidable disparities that, although notably alleviated in the period from 1945 to 1969, were still fairly conspicuous. As an example, illiteracy was abolished in Slovenia at the time of World War II, and the centenary of compulsory eight-year education was celebrated in Slovenia in 1969.

---

*The six republics include Serbia, Macedonia, Bosnia-Herzegovina, Montenegro, Croatia, and Slovenia. The Yugoslav state is of comparatively recent origin, having been established in 1918 after the end of World War I. According to the 1961 population census, the "nationalities" in Yugoslavia included Albanians, 914,000; Hungarians, 504,000; Turks, 183,000; Slovaks, 86,000; Bulgarians, 63,000; Romanians, 61,000; Czechs, 30,000; and Italians, 26,000. The term "nationalities" is used to distinguish these groups.

Our data on levels of education in Belgrade and Ljubljana reflect these discrepancies. Belgrade, the capital of Serbia, shows a substantial number of respondents who had less than an eighth-grade education. The data also reflect more substantially another distinctive condition—an almost overwhelming wave of migration into Belgrade, most of it from smaller towns and surrounding peasantry. Sociologists have referred to this as the "ruralization of Belgrade." Ljubljana, the center of culture of Slovenia, has been less subject to rural influences.

One must contrast these Old World cultures with that of Seattle, a city of about 500,000 population, which goes back not much more than a century and of which little remains that marked its origins. Seattle is essentially a late-nineteenth and twentieth century community, with a mixed ethnic character made up largely of Scandinavians, English, Irish, and with a compound of European, Asian, and Russian influences. It is a shipping and sophisticated manufacturing center, with the Boeing company its largest employer, complemented by supportive industries,

Seattle is a seaport as well, which distinguishes it in other ways from Ljubljana and Belgrade. It is a sea and air transportation hub for Alaska and Asia. There is some affinity with Ljubljana in this respect for, while Seattle is remote from other areas in terms of miles, it is an active transportation center and a good proportion of its own literate population travels abroad. Ljubljana is in the same sense close to Central Europe and Italy.

Speaking of differences in culture among the Yugoslav republics, the UNESCO report asserts that, despite great efforts, the development of national cultures is still fairly uneven in Yugoslavia. Some of these discrepancies were reflected in our audience data, particularly with regard to education and the distribution of skills across the population.

The UNESCO data on media growth in Yugoslavia are indicative of rates of economic and social development. In an eight-year period, holdings of books in scientific and technical libraries increased by 50 percent, and the number of books issued by libraries increased at a slightly greater ratio. The total number of books in public libraries almost doubled, while the number of books issued increased about 60 percent. Publishing houses went from approximately 5,500 to almost 10,000 in a seven-year period from 1961 to 1968, with the total distribution of volumes more than doubling from 33 to 68 million.

Radio subscribers and stations increased even more dramatically during this period. The number of radio stations increased from 19 to 94 (most of these were local stations) and the number of subscribers (usually an underestimation of sets in use) tripled. The number of hours on the air also doubled during this period.

There was one radio for every two households in Yugoslavia in 1968. The average in Slovenia (with a higher figure for Ljubljana) was one per household. The ratio in Serbia was one radio set per two households, with higher figures for Belgrade. This does not include sales of transistors, of which half a million were sold in 1968.

With respect to television, the increases have been remarkable. There were 6,000 television sets in Yugoslavia in 1958; ten years later there were 1.3 million. In 1969 the total increased by another 250,000; it is likely that in 1970, at the time of our study, the total had reached 2 million.

UNESCO reported that in 1968 a total of 63 percent of Yugoslavia was covered by television networks and that 86 percent of the population was able to view television in this area.

The ratio of television sets per household was one to every four households in 1968; this was 1 to 3 in Slovenia and 1 to 4.4 in Serbia. However, the figures were considerably different in Ljubljana and Belgrade, the capital cities—probably closer to 1 to 2 in Ljubljana and 1 to 3 in Belgrade.

These statistics are somewhat confused, however, by the unreflected but high rate of group viewing, particularly among members of the same family but different (often nearby) households. It is probable that only the very old in the city and the isolated in the countryside (many more of the latter) now lack access to a television set.

In Television 1967 a study in Slovenia, by Kroflić et al., some 49 percent of those in the city and surrounding areas of Ljubljana were found to have television sets. (All the following figures come from Kroflić et al., Television 1967; see Bibliography.) The number of viewers per television set was significantly greater than the number of sets. About half the sets played to three to four persons, while another 30 percent played to five or more persons. Only 20 percent played to only one or two persons.

The study showed that 34 percent of those who did not own a television set nonetheless watched television. However, their frequency of viewing was sharply less than the viewing of those who did own television sets.

The study also showed that a greater number of "guests" watching television correlated with lower education. Only 5 percent of those of higher education reported four or more guest viewers for their sets, compared to 35 percent for those of lowest levels of education and 20 percent for those of secondary school levels of education. Stated in terms of averages, an average of four persons per set watched television owned by those of lower education, compared to 3.4 and 3.0 for those of secondary and higher education.

Although only 23 percent of those of grade school education owned a television set in Slovenia, some 35 percent watched television. While

48 percent of the grade school level craftsmen owned television sets, 65 percent said they watched TV. Some 70 percent of the secondary education group owned TV but 80 percent watched; 68 percent of those of higher education owned TV sets but 82 percent were viewers.

A mass media factor of some importance is the geographical setting of Ljubljana as compared to Belgrade. Ljubljana is placed so that it has easy access to Austrian and Italian radio and television by both regular and shortwave radio and both VHF and UHF television transmissions. Added to this are such cultural factors as language commonalities (a great deal of Italian and Austrian-German is spoken in Ljubljana) and the ethnic imprints from long-time Austrian influences and World War II occupation by Italy.

Seattle has access to Canadian television and radio, almost to the same extent as Ljubljana to Italian and Austrian television.

The study of television in Slovenia in 1967 showed that 27 percent of set owners technically could view Austrian television and 21 percent Italian television, while 22 percent could view television from Zagreb, the capital of Croatia. This would not be the case for Belgrade.

A later, 1969, study of Slovenia showed that approximately 15 percent actually watched Italian television at least "occasionally" and 14 percent watched Austrian television, a total of 29 percent exposure to outside channels. (The subsequent figures come from the 1969 study, Slovensko, Javno Mnenje, 1969.)

For all of Slovenia, there was a correlation of education with watching foreign television news. Those of secondary and higher education watched more Italian news than did those of lower education. Interestingly, however, there was no difference for Austrian television. One reason, apparently, was that areas closer to Austria tended to be more rural and small-town, where levels of education might be lower, but nationalities were more closely linked.

In response to a question as to the need for listening to foreign radio broadcasts and reading the foreign press, 76 percent of the white-collar class, compared to 58 percent of the blue-collar and 42 percent of the peasant class, in Slovenia said that such listening and reading was necessary. These and other figures on use of foreign media appear to reflect cultural factors. In this context, approximately one-third of the public said that they listened to foreign radio broadcasts for information about public affairs.

THE MEDIA ENVIRONMENT

A related question with respect to media availabilities was not whether one community offered greater or lesser varieties of media but whether an individual of given education, age, or knowledge might find adequate sources to meet his needs. The answer to this question was less to be found in the number of media than in the use and evaluation of media sources and content.

Nonetheless, we will sketch the media environments of the three cities to provide some picture of media availabilities as such. It can be observed that the three communities are in many respects comparable in the availability of local press, television, and radio.

Belgrade

Belgrade has four daily newspapers, two morning and two afternoon. The morning dailies are _Politika_ and _Borba_. _Politika_ has a daily circulation of 270,000. Once a party newspaper, _Borba_ is now a general circulation daily of 31,000 circulation. Both newspapers cover a spectrum of world and local public affairs, cultural, and social affairs.

The two evening newspapers are _Politika Ekspres_, published by the _Politika_ House, and _Vecernje Novosti_, which is part of the _Borba_ House. _Politika Ekspres_ has a daily circulation of about 207,000 while _Vecernje Novosti_ has the largest circulation in Belgrade, some 379,000. Each of these newspapers carries a small amount of local, regional, national, and world news, but they emphasize human interest, popularized content. Called "amusement" content, these newspapers stress accidents, crime, sex, and personalities.

In Belgrade, the weekly magazine _NIN_ is considered a part of the press. It is published by _Politika_ and devotes a good deal of its content to discussions of local and world affairs, commentary, and so forth. It is similar in style to the weekly magazines in the Sunday editions of American newspapers, but it is more extensive in content. _Illustrated Politika_ has a circulation of about 250,000 weekly; it contains some general information but is popular in its appeal, in the pattern of the afternoon daily newspapers.

At the time of this study, Belgrade had only one television channel. In the past year, it has added another channel. This is similar but has more commercial content.

The first news shows come on at 5 p.m. and are broadcast in the languages of smaller ethnic groups (Hungarian and Albanian) in the Belgrade area. The news content is similar to that broadcast later.

At 6 p.m. the first general newscasts begin. These last for 15 to 20 minutes and are devoted to both local and world news. At 7 p.m. there are additional short newscasts devoted largely to local news.

At 8 p.m. the most important news program is broadcast. It covers both local and world political affairs and some local social affairs. Part of this is in the form of remotes and minidocumentaries; the rest are reports by newsmen. There is a late news show at the end of broadcasting for the day, which may vary in time from 10 p.m. to later, depending on the nature of the earlier programming.

Once a week there is a special program of about one hour, "Reflektor," that describes local political and social problems; a counterpart program, now called "Krug," appears on the new second channel and covers world affairs. A serial program, "The Time Machine," covers matters of interest in a historical context. A TV mail program permits audiences to ask questions about a variety of matters, including public and world affairs problems.

It is estimated that about 80 percent of those in Belgrade have access to television sets, either through ownership (about 60 percent) or viewing (another 20 percent).

There are two major programs or channels on Belgrade radio. Belgrade I goes on the air at 4 a.m. daily and broadcasts until midnight. Belgrade II is on the air from 12 noon to 9 p.m. It is followed immediately by Belgrade III, educational radio, which generally broadcasts until 12 midnight. On Friday night Belgrade II continues to 4 a.m. for youth, incorporating pop music and a disk jockey format.

About every two hours Belgrade I and II broadcast short news shows, about 5 to 10 minutes in duration. The evening radio news shows run approximately 10 to 20 minutes. The two stations are similar in that they both cover a wide range of music, concerts, drama, and news content. Belgrade III carries serious music, discussions, and cultural content.

Belgrade 202 is one of two pop stations. The other is sponsored by _Borba_ House and is called "Studio B."

There is almost complete distribution of radio sets in households in Belgrade.

Ljubljana

Ljubljana has two morning daily newspapers, _Delo_ and _Dnevnik._ _Delo_ is in many respects the counterpart of _Politika_. It maintains correspondents abroad and in other regions of Yugoslavia. It has wide coverage of foreign affairs and internal Yugoslav affairs as well. It has diversified content, much more so than _Dnevnik_, which is more local than cosmopolitan in its content. _Delo_ has a circulation of approximately 93,500, while _Dnevnik_ has a smaller circulation of 67,000. _Dnevnik_ much more resembles a local newspaper, carrying a modest degree of foreign and national news.

Ljubljana also has a number of weekly newspapers and magazines. _Tedenska Tribune_ is a general-circulation Sunday news weekly, comparable to *NIN* in Belgrade; it contains political, social, and other news and commentary. *NIN*, however, is more of a magazine in format. (*NIN* is also distributed in Ljubljana.) *Tovaris* emphasizes internal problems of self-management, the economy, and similar topics. *Zvatorepec* is a satirical magazine. It is similar to *Jez* in Belgrade. Ljubljana has its own array of special-interest magazines devoted to personalities, television, sports, and what might be called popular themes. Most of these weeklies have small circulations, between 1,500 and 2,000 copies, with the exception of the "popular" weekly media, which have large circulations.

The television and radio outlets in Ljubljana very closely follow the pattern in Belgrade, part of a national pattern of a single television channel and two major radio stations. Ljubljana has also acquired a second TV channel; it was the first to engage in color transmission.

Seattle

Seattle has two daily newspapers, the *Times* and the *Post-Intelligencer*. The *Times* is an independent conservative afternoon newspaper with a circulation of 230,439 daily and 288,257 on Sundays. The *Post-Intelligencer* is a Hearst newspaper but carries columnists and the news service of the New York *Times*. Its circulation is 182,192 daily and 242,490 Sundays. Neither newspaper carries a great deal of world news; each is fairly typical for its size circulation. Seattle is largely a professional community, with several universities and advanced technology industries such as the Boeing company.

There are three network television stations, the CBS, ABC, and NBC outlets. Each carries all of the network documentaries, special public affairs programs, and morning, early evening, and late evening news shows. In addition, each station attempts to do a full job of covering local news.

Seattle also has an educational television station, Channel 9, which carries local discussion and public affairs shows and the network offerings of the Public Broadcasting Service. In addition, those who subscribe to a cable service also are able to obtain news shows from Channel 12 in Vancouver, British Columbia (Canada), and Channels 11 and 13 from Tacoma. Channel 12 is also a CBS network outlet and duplicates most of the content of Channel 7 in Seattle.

There are 17 regular broadcast radio stations in Seattle, several of which are specialty stations that broadcast almost exclusively religious news and commentary and popular music. The news radio stations are primarily network-affiliated. Some also are on limited broadcast schedules. However, it is also possible to hear stations from nearby communities.

Radio news typically consists of numerous short broadcasts, similar in pattern to what is broadcast on Yugoslav radio. But there is somewhat less content devoted to news commentary than on Yugoslav radio.

Overall, there appeared to be a high degree of availability of all media in the three cultures. A variety of press, television, radio, film, and library resources were accessible.

PART

II

ARRAYS OF THE DATA

CHAPTER

5

THE SOCIAL STRUCTURE

Our first step in assessing our findings was to note the distribution of responses to our questions in each city. We needed to examine the distributions of values across such variables as education, income, and age to determine if our methodology had permitted the variance in behavior that we might expect.

Our first look at the data was not intended to compare the three cities but rather to permit a description of each city. We did not wish to compare cities themselves but rather to compare equivalent social groupings across cities. As examples:

Ljubljana had the greatest proportion of long-time residents and Seattle the greatest proportion of short-time residents.

Ljubljana reflected the highest rate of employment, some 63 percent, followed by Belgrade and Seattle. These seemingly surprising figures were apparently a product of greater female employment in the Yugoslav cities and the temporary conditions of unemployment that existed in Seattle at the time of the study. To some extent, also, Yugoslavs at this time were taking jobs in Western Europe and elsewhere. Most of these persons, however, came from rural areas and smaller towns.

Seattle showed the highest level of education because of fewer persons at the lowest educational levels. Ljubljana's pattern was more like that of Belgrade in its incidence of those with eighth-grade but not lesser education. The university level of education was fairly equally distributed across the three cities.

The Seattle distribution of income was much more even across the population, while Belgrade's was concentrated in the lower-income groupings. Ljubljana also weighted toward lower income levels, but fell midway between Seattle and Belgrade.

The Seattle distribution of age was weighted toward the younger groupings somewhat more than Belgrade and Ljubljana.

Seattle reported a significantly greater proportion of married couples, which might also help to explain the employment distribution noted earlier (fewer married women work), while the Belgrade and Ljubljana figures were very similar.

A slightly greater number of males were reported in the Seattle sample. This could be a product of special Yugoslav experience.

These demographics illustrated substantial differences among the three cultures. Given these differences, we also looked for differences in decision-making and communication behaviors. These are assessed independently for local and world problems in the following chapters.

TABLE 5.1

The Social Structure
(percentages)

Demographic	Belgrade	Ljubljana	Seattle
Years of residence			
0-5	6	5	21
6-10	23	19	17
11-15	34	29	24
15	37	47	38
Employed	53	63	46
Unemployed	36-47	37	54
Educational level			
Primary	30.1	24.6	17.4
Secondary	49.4	56.0	57.8
University	20.5	10.4	24.8
Income level			
First level[a]	63	44	15
Second level[b]	32	44	15
Third level[c]	5	12	8
Fourth level[d]			62
Age level			
Up to 29	21	20	33
30-59	63	60	43
60+	16	20	23
Married	85	79	80
Unmarried	15	21	20
Male	44	45	47
Female	56	55	53

[a]First level — Belgrade and Ljubljana: 1,000 ND; Seattle: $5,000.

[b]Second level — Belgrade and Ljubljana: 2,000 ND; Seattle: $10,000.

[c]Third level — Belgrade and Ljubljana: 3,000 + ND; Seattle: $15,000.

[d]Fourth level — Seattle : $15,000 +.

CHAPTER

6

KNOWLEDGE AND DECISION-MAKING

How should such factors as variations in education, income, age, and sex roles affect knowledge and decision-making in the three cultures about a variety of local and world problems?

LOCAL PROBLEMS

We had developed seven measures of knowledge and decision-making.

1. Number of important local problems: Seattle named the most local problems, followed by Belgrade and then Ljubljana. Greater income and education, it is easy to hypothesize, should produce more awareness of local problems. The fact that, despite these factors, Belgrade proposed a great number of local problems suggested that some special situational or cultural factors were at work.

2. Number of reasons for local problems being important: More of those in Seattle gave more reasons for problems being important, followed by Belgrade. Apparently, local problems in Seattle and Belgrade were more salient to the individual than in Ljubljana.

3. Comparing one problem to another: Despite having named more local problems, and giving more reasons for their importance, respondents in Seattle were less likely to compare one local problem to another. We speculated that this might be because of the special nature of the most important problem to most Seattleites—unemployment. Those in Belgrade engaged in more comparisons than did respondents in either Seattle or Ljubljana, indicating possible linkage of local problems. However, we have no other evidence to test this assumption.

4. Description of the local problem without regard to other problems: The concern of Seattleites with the single local problem of employment was reflected by the degree to which they described the local problem without regard to other local problems. By contrast, there were no differences in behavior between Belgrade and Ljubljana.

5. Description of the local problem as important to oneself, personally: Consistent with what has been observed, there was a somewhat greater tendency for those in Seattle to identify the local problem as personal.

6. Description of the local problem by restatement: Respondents in each of the three communities were similar in their tendency to restate a problem as a way of describing its importance. This suggests an inability on the part of those individuals to define the problems in terms that permitted solutions.

7. Number of solutions to local problems: Seattle proposed more problems, and more Seattle respondents were able to propose more solutions. Looking at this as a proportion of problems suggested, however, there were few differences among respondents in the three communities.

WORLD PROBLEMS

We assumed that there would be a different picture for world problems. Where Belgrade was more attuned to local problems, we expected Ljubljana to be more concerned about world problems. Seattle, we hypothesized, would be attuned as much to world problems as to local problems.

1. Number of world problems: Actually, those in Seattle named many more world problems, followed by Ljubljana and then Belgrade. Seattle respondents named more problems—local and world—of all kinds.

2. Number of reasons for problems being important: There were no significant differences among communities in the ability of respondents to tell why problems were important.

3. Comparing one problem to another: Those in Ljubljana and Belgrade were more likely to compare one world problem to another as a means of describing the importance of a problem. More than in Seattle they perceived linkage of world problems.

4. Describing the problem without regard to other problems: There was a tendency in Seattle to describe one world problem—Vietnam—without regard to other world problems. Those in Ljubljana and Belgrade apparently were concerned with problems of war and peace in more abstract—and common—terms.

5. Description of the problem as important to oneself, personally: The implications of Vietnam were present again in the stronger tendency for Seattle respondents to describe world problems as important because they were personally affected.

6. Restatement of the problem: There were few tendencies in each of the three communities to employ restatement as an attribute for a world problem. In this sense, individuals were more articulate about world problems than about local problems.

7. Number of solutions for world problems: There was little difference across cultures in the ability to provide solutions for world problems. Seattle respondents were somewhat more solution-minded, and Belgrade respondents were least solution-minded, but not to a significant degree.

TABLE 6.1

Knowledge and Decision-Making: Local Problems
(percentages)

Variable	Belgrade					Ljubljana					Seattle				
	0	1	2	3	4	0	1	2	3	4	0	1	2	3	4
Number of local problems		12	20	30	38		21	19	25	35		10	15	21	54
Number of local solutions		52	28	10	10		54	27	11	8		47	26	14	13
Compares one problem to another	44	56				71	29				83	17			
Attribute for only one problem	86	14			88	12			52	48					
Problem is important to self	59	41			55	45			46	54					
Restates problem without attribute	92	8				93	7				88	12			
Reasons why problem is important	8	66	25	1		19	70	11			14	34	37	15	

TABLE 6.2

Knowledge and Decision-Making: World Problems
(percentages)

Variable	Belgrade				Ljubljana				Seattle			
	1	2	3	4	1	2	3	4	1	2	3	4
Number of world problems	28	28	27	17	21	22	26	31	11	18	20	51
Number of world solutions	58	25	7	10	51	27	11	11	51	25	13	11
	No	Yes			No	Yes			No	Yes		
Compares one problem to another	48	52			57	43			71	29		
Attribute for only one problem	76	24			83	17			49	51		
Problem is important to self	82	18			76	24			65	35		
Restates problem without attribute	86	14			87	13			91	9		
Reasons why problem is important	17	83			20	80			21	79		

CHAPTER

7 USE AND EVALUATION OF COMMUNICATION

A number of media and communication variables had been developed. Respondents had been asked how they learned about the local problem and if they had discussed it with anyone either in an interpersonal or group setting. They also were asked if they wished to have more information.

Media sources included television, radio, and the press. Other sources included motion pictures, books, and school. Interpersonal sources included family and friends. But the most significant source of knowledge about local problems was personal observation.

LOCAL PROBLEMS

Media Use

Seattle and Belgrade had reported the most local problems and more knowledge about those problems. Therefore, it was to be expected that they would cite more sources of information about those problems. Let us look at this by media:

Television: Seattle reported television much more as a source of information about local problems, followed by Belgrade and then Ljubljana.

Radio: Seattle also reported radio more as a source of information; Belgrade and Ljubljana were similar in their lesser use of radio.

Press: Seattle reported significantly more that the press was a source of information about local problems, followed again by Belgrade and Ljubljana.

Movies: There was little use of movies and little variation across the three cities.

Books: There was a greater use of books in Seattle, but the utility of books as a source was not great. Nor were books significant for Belgrade or Ljubljana.

School: Almost the same findings held for use of schools as for books.

Friends: There was somewhat greater use of friends as a source of information in Seattle, followed by Belgrade and Ljubljana.

Family: There also was greater use of the family as a source of information in Seattle, followed again by Belgrade and Ljubljana, but the extent of use of the family as a source of information was not great.

Local meetings: There was a greater number of reports of local meetings as a source of information about local problems in Seattle; there were no differences in this respect between Belgrade and Ljubljana. Evidently, self-management enterprises in Yugoslavia do not absorb themselves with community problems but deal primarily with their own problems.

Personal experience: There were more reports of personal involvement in local problems in Belgrade, followed by Seattle and Ljubljana. This was despite the finding that more local problems were reported in Seattle.

With respect to interpersonal discussion, discussion at local meetings, and wanting information, there were these results:

- There was more interpersonal discussion in Seattle and Ljubljana than in Belgrade. Apparently, more individuals in Ljubljana engaged in discussion about fewer problems. This could be a situational factor or related to social structure.
- There were no differences in reports of discussion at local meetings. As suggested earlier, this is interesting in view of the emphasis placed on self-management in Yugoslavia.
- There was a greater desire expressed for more information in Ljubljana than in Belgrade or Seattle. This implied a greater belief in the efficacy of information for understanding and solving problems.

In summary, our expectations for differences in the utility of media and interpersonal communication followed from our data on knowledge and decision-making.

Media Evaluation

Respondents also were asked which sources of information were most useful and least useful, and why.

Most useful sources: The press was named as most useful in each city, somewhat more so in Ljubljana, followed by Belgrade and

Seattle. Television was named next most useful. Radio was named very seldom as most useful.

Least useful: All media were more or less equally named least useful in all three cities. Radio was least valued.

Why most useful: In Belgrade, the local source was most useful because of its availability; in Ljubljana, it was a matter of content and availability; in Seattle, it was valued because of channel dimensionalities and content. In all three cities, trust was deemed the least pertinent reason for valuing a source of information. This raises substantial questions about the efficacy and conditions of appropriateness of this variable for research in mass communication.

Why source least useful: In all three cities, the source of news was deemed to be least useful first because of a lack of availability, and second because of its content. The least pertinent reasons for lack of source utility included trust and channel dimensionalities.

Of great interest was the fact that content, accessibility, and channel dimensionalities were significant in that order, while trust or credibility was by far the least significant.

Respondents were asked to evaluate each of the media. The profiles that emerged showed that the press was judged to be most useful for local problems because of its content, television to be most useful because of its channel dimensionalities, and radio to be most useful because of its accessibility as a source of information. These relationships were similar across the three communities.

WORLD PROBLEMS

Media Use

Since world problems were less subject to personal observation and validation, we expected greater utilization for media use and communication. However, Seattle respondents did not use more media sources for world problems than for local problems. The implications are that local problems are as "abstract" and of as great a concern in Seattle as world problems are.

Television: There was greater use of television in Ljubljana and Belgrade for world problems, than for local problems, but, Seattle tended only slightly more to use television as a source of information for world problems.

Radio: There was increased use of radio in all three communities. Ljubljana used radio most, followed by Belgrade and Seattle.

Press: There was sharply increased use of the press in Ljubljana and Belgrade, for world problems but in Seattle the same level of press use was maintained. Overall, there were no differences across the three communities in the use of the press. This had not been the case for local problems.

Movies: There was somewhat greater use of movies in Belgrade and Ljubljana for world problems; there was little use of movies as a source in Seattle.

Books: There was greatly increased use of books, particularly in Seattle and Ljubljana.

School: There was greater use of the school in Belgrade and Ljubljana; Seattle maintained the same utility.

Friends: There was greater use of friends in Seattle, followed by Ljubljana and then Belgrade. Generally, there was less use of friends as a source of information about world problems than about local problems.

Family: There was only slightly greater use of family as a source of information in Seattle, and there were no differences between Belgrade and Ljubljana.

Meetings: Seattle demonstrated more utility for meetings than Belgrade and Ljubljana, but in absolute terms there was no more use of meetings than had been the case for local problems.

Personal experience: There were few differences across communities in utility of personal experience as a source of information about world problems. And there were fewer references to personal experience.

Turning to interpersonal communication, we had these findings:

- There was more discussion of world problems in Seattle and Ljubljana than in Belgrade.
- There was also slightly more discussion of world problems at meetings in Seattle and Ljubljana than in Belgrade.
- The same pattern—Seattle, Ljubljana, Belgrade—was followed with respect to wanting, or believing in the efficacy of, more information.

Overall there was substantially more use of the press and television than of other media as sources of information.

In comparative terms, Seattle did not use media differently for world problems than for local problems, while in Belgrade and Ljubljana there was substantially greater media utilization for world problems.

Movies, books, and school were not useful sources for local problems, but they had some utility for world problems.

Respondents in all three cities were more knowledgeable about world problems and used more sources of information as a basis for that knowledge. They also engaged in more interpersonal communication and discussion at meetings and were more actively engaged in a search for information.

Media Evaluation

Turning to the evaluation of media sources, we had expected that, since world problems were more abstract, there would be different bases for judging the utility of media.

Most useful world source: Television emerged as a more useful source for world problems than for local problems, but the press still was judged most useful.

Least useful world source: Television was judged much less often to be least useful; radio was judged most often to be least useful.

Why world source most useful: As compared with local problems, media sources in Seattle were judged more on content and less on availability. In Belgrade and Ljubljana, by contrast, greater attention was given to channel dimensionalities.

Why world soruce least useful: The pattern of utility did not shift in any consistent or significant way from local to world problems.

How were each of the media themselves judged with respect to utility for world problems?

Television was more judged on the basis of channel dimensionalities for world problems than for local problems. As expressed by many of our respondents, "one could see it as it happened." Otherwise, there were no differences in media utilities other than had been observed for local problems.

TABLE 7.1

Media Use and Communication: Local Problems
(percentages)

Variable	Belgrade				Ljubljana				Seattle			
	Yes	No			Yes	No			Yes	No		
Discussed problem	76	24			87	13			87	13		
Attended meeting	34	66			32	68			33	67		
Wanted more information	53	47			63	37			55	45		
Mentioned TV	62	38			68	32			38	62		
Mentioned radio	75	25			73	27			61	39		
Mentioned press	46	54			54	46			25	75		
Mentioned movie	98	2			97	3			96	4		
Mentioned book	97	3			96	4			91	9		
Mentioned school	96	4			97	3			88	12		
Mentioned friend	59	41			68	32			49	51		
Mentioned family	89	11			92	8			82	18		
Mentioned personal experience	13	87			17	83			37	63		
Number of source attributes for most useful	34	66			48	52			20	80		
Number of sources for local problems	1	2	3	4	1	2	3	4	1	2	3	4
	31	17	19	33	42	11	16	31	13	11	23	53

TABLE 7.2

Media Use and Communication: World Problems
(percentages)

Variable	Belgrade				Ljubljana				Seattle			
	Yes	No			Yes	No			Yes	No		
Discussed problem	76	24			87	13			85	15		
Attended meeting	40	60			36	64			36	64		
Wanted more information	44	56			48	52			50	50		
Mentioned TV	38	62			34	66			32	68		
Mentioned radio	49	51			36	64			55	45		
Mentioned press	27	73			22	78			23	77		
Mentioned movie	86	14			82	18			94	6		
Mentioned book	87	13			80	20			78	22		
Mentioned school	87	13			87	13			81	19		
Mentioned friend	73	27			66	34			58	42		
Mentioned family	87	13			87	13			83	17		
Mentioned meeting	86	14			85	15			74	26		
Mentioned personal experience	60	40			55	45			53	47		
Number of source attributes termed most useful	1	2	3+		1	2	3+		1	2	3+	
	25	55	19		27	54	17		18	60	22	
Number of sources for world problems	1	2	3	4	1	2	3	4	1	2	3	4
	24	11	21	44	21	6	17	56	14	11	23	52

TABLE 7.3

Media Preference For Local Problems
(percentages)

	Belgrade			Ljubljana			Seattle		
	TV	Radio	Press	TV	Radio	Press	TV	Radio	Press
Most Useful Local Source	30	4 (N=306)	65	26	3 (N=207)	71	32	7 (N=324)	61
Least Useful Local Source	32	36 (N=269)	32	25	39 (N=159)	36	29	36 (N=324)	35

TABLE 7.4

Media Evaluation on Local Problems
(percentages)

	Belgrade			Ljubljana			Seattle		
	TV	Radio	Press	TV	Radio	Press	TV	Radio	Press
Why Most Useful									
Trust	7.5	0	14.2	2.6	0	8.3	8.9	10.0	7.1
Availability	16.4	46.7	16.9	28.9	80.0	30.6	31.1	45.0	20.1
Cognitive	23.9	33.3	58.1	23.7	20.0	55.6	38.9	40.0	58.6
Channel	52.2	20.0	10.8	44.7	0	5.6	21.1	5.0	14.2

TABLE 7.5

Media Preference For World Problems
(percentages)

	Belgrade			Ljubljana			Seattle		
	TV	Radio	Press	TV	Radio	Press	TV	Radio	Press
Most Useful Source	46	5	49	37	9	54	40	3	57
		(N=603)			(N=486)			(N=372)	
Least Useful Source	17	63	20	16	54	30	20	43	37
		(N=261)			(N=184)			(N=256)	

TABLE 7.6

Media Evaluation On World Problems
(percentages)

	Belgrade			Ljubljana			Seattle		
	TV	Radio	Press	TV	Radio	Press	TV	Radio	Press
Why Most Useful									
Trust	5.7	12.5	12.9	3.1	5.3	8.1	7.6	12.5	5.7
Availability	10.3	45.6	22.0	27.6	71.1	36.4	24.4	75.0	21.7
Cognitive	10.3	25.0	59.1	13.4	18.4	51.7	22.9	0	56.0
Channel	73.7	16.7	6.0	55.9	5.3	3.8	45.0	12.5	16.6

PART

III

DEMOGRAPHIC ANALYSES

CHAPTER

8 EDUCATION AND LOCAL PROBLEMS

We expected differences among educational groupings but we did not expect the differences to be dramatic in scope.* The reason was methodological. Our respondents had been permitted to discuss problems that were of importance to them, personally. We had not imposed upon our respondents irrelevant problems that required highly adaptive behavior. Hence we could expect lower education groups to respond more effectively to these problems than to problems with which they were unfamiliar and which demanded greater adaptability.

The earlier Yugoslav research on education and media use had utilized more conventional methodological approaches. As a result, it reflected strong patterns of association between education and media use and evaluation.

BELGRADE

Background

A few studies and their concerns are illustrative. Danojlić (1969a) asked about readership of daily and weekly newspapers and

---

*Educational levels were treated as three categories—low, moderate, and high. The high category included university students as well as graduates of higher schools and universities. However, in Yugoslavia the gymnasium level of education is equivalent to junior-college level in Seattle. Therefore, we placed "some college" respondents in Seattle in the "middle" group rather than in the "high" education group.

found a very high correlation between education and reading. The differences between educational groups were startling. Some 83 percent of those who attended no school said they read no newspapers of any kind, a much higher figure than we will present. Illustrative of the methodological problem, two-thirds said they "could not read," but this was a self-assessment. The uneducated person was required to adapt his response to terms used by the researcher—for example, an "occasional" or "rare" reader.

In a similar study, Bacević (1965a) found that education correlated very highly with the reading of periodicals. Exposure to television also was strongly correlated with education. Bacević (1965b) also found that the audiences for the mass media were differentiated primarily at the secondary level of education, with more use of all mass media at that level and less at the university level. This was the only such study reporting this finding, one that will find corroboration in our data. It is suggestive of elitist tendencies to reduce dependence on mass media.

In all of these studies, there was an overwhelmingly high correlation of education and media exposure, so high as to suggest that education was more highly attitudinal self-estimates of media exposure rather than reports of actual behavior.

Yugoslav studies borrowed questions from the American Roper studies conducted for the Television Information Office. In response to the question, "Which of the media would you be <u>least</u> willing to give up?" the more educated the respondent, the less the person was willing to give up the press and the more willing to give up radio. Television at this time was not a factor.

Asked which media they "preferred," Danoljić (1965b) reported that those of higher education were much more likely to prefer the press, while those of lower education were even more likely to prefer radio. Thus, the illiterate and the college-educated both were less likely to prefer television. The illiterates apparently were affected by less availability of television, while those of highest education apparently found television less useful, although available.

Those of the highest education also were most able to offer criticisms of the press. However, the nature of criticism did not differ across educational levels with regard to use of such criteria as informational content or trustworthiness. Our data will raise questions about these findings. However, those of higher education expressed more comments about the lack of utility of content, a finding that is more in keeping with our data.

When Bacević (1965a) asked respondents what the media "meant" to them, there appeared to be little difference by educational levels, curiously enough. Nonetheless, across media, the press was much more cited as a source of information. In part, this will prove consistent with our findings.

Finally, in asking about first, second, and third degrees of loyalty to a medium, Leandrov (1967) also discovered that those of the highest education were least likely to wish to give up the press. Television was the most valued source for those of middle education, while radio was the most useful to those of lowest education. These findings will receive some corroboration in our data.

Findings

Let us turn now to our own findings.

We expected that more of those of the highest levels of education would be knowledgeable and able to use that knowledge in making decisions about problems. More of those of higher education were, indeed, able to propose more local problems, more attributes, and more solutions for those problems.

More of those of higher education also were likely to compare one problem to another, and to distinguish problems by use of attributes. They were less likely to use "self" as an attribute; that is, they were not likely to say that the problem was important merely because it was important to them, personally. Thus our expectations for decision-making were confirmed with respect to levels of education.

We looked for corresponding differences in media use and communication. As expected, more of those of higher education used a greater number of sources of information, including more television, press, friends, and references to personal experience. But there were no differences in the use of radio across educational levels. Thus radio was not a very discriminating medium.

While those of lower education had less access to media and to persons as sources of information, they nonetheless were nearly as likely to express a need for information. The essential problem for those of lower education appeared to be an ability to use information.

The greatest differences were between those of the lowest and combined middle-higher education groups. But many of those of lower education (approximately a third), including the "nonliterate," were nonetheless attentive to all media. Contrary to the Yugoslav media research for Belgrade, the differences between educational groups were significant but not overwhelming or dramatic. There was substantial use of print and television at all educational levels and only somewhat less use of radio by the least educated.

With respect to media evaluation, more of those of higher education named the press as most useful, while more of those of lower education cited personal experience. Television also was more likely to be cited by those of lower education.

The bases for judging the usefulness of sources of information differed by level of education. Those of the highest education tended to cite elements of content, while those of lower education cited the availability or accessibility of media sources. The latter were less discriminating, non-content relevant responses, we concluded. To our surprise, there were no appreciable differences across educational levels in references to trust or channel characteristics as criteria for evaluating media. But this was for local problems, which could be observed directly by the individual.

LJUBLJANA

Background

The early research on media ownership, use, and evaluation is centered on three major studies conducted in Slovenia. Most of the data that we are reporting come from the Institute of Sociology, Radio 1967, and Kroflič et al., Television 1967, studies conducted by the Institute for Social Sciences in Ljubljana, and from Vreg's Study of Mass Communication, 1969, conducted by the Higher School for Political Science, Sociology, and Journalism, Center for Mass Communication and Public Opinion. The Ljubljana picture must be extrapolated in many instances from the Slovenian data where it is not reported separately. In such cases, the Ljubljana figures—representing the most sophisticated urban center in Slovenia—would be significantly higher.

Overall, there was more use of radio and television in Slovenia reported in these early studies than we observed for Belgrade, while use of the press was comparable. This reflects the difference in patterns of media use in the two cities that our data will reveal.

Radio and television ownership was higher in Slovenia than in Belgrade. Approximately 70 percent of those with secondary school education and over had television sets compared to 48 percent for grade school-level skilled craftsmen and only 23 percent for those of lower education who were unskilled workers, according to Television 1967.

The same study found that only 41 percent of the low education respondents had both a radio and a TV set in their homes. Those with only a grade school education but in the professional trades were more likely to own both a television set and a radio (66 percent), while the highest figures were for the secondary and over secondary, at 77 and 72 percent. Ljubljana, as an urban center, represented substantially higher percentages than for Slovenia as a whole, but we do not have the precise breakdowns.

Interestingly, those of the highest education had owned their television sets for the longest period of time—more than five years at that time.

Looking at radio audiences, Radio 1967 showed that 84 percent of those with up to eight years of school, compared with 91 to 95 percent in the higher grades, said that they listened to radio, a saturation figure. However, our data for radio listening with respect to a specific, important problem will show a much lower figure.

In the Slovensko 1969 study, there were few differences across educational levels; in fact, those of lower education were somewhat more likely to refer to themselves as radio listeners. A 1971 commercial study showed that those of higher education tended slightly less to listen to the radio but considerably more to watch television, doubtless a question of economic access to television.

The 1967 Slovenia study showed that those of grade school level who were unskilled were the least exposed to television. Those of grade school education in the skilled occupations and those with secondary education were the most frequent viewers, but those of higher education watched television news more often and preferred it to other television content.

With respect to newspapers, those of higher education generally tended more to read Delo than did those of lower education. This was true to a lesser extent for Dnevnik, but was not true for Vecer. Comparing those of different levels of education, a general relationship was found between reading Delo, the Borba House newspaper, and education.

Respondents were asked the American Roper poll question as to which medium of communication they would least like to give up. Those of higher education most wished to keep television, followed by radio and newspapers; peasants, housewives, and retired persons wished most to keep radio and then television and newspapers. Those of lower education preferred radio, followed by television and newspapers. These figures were affected by the availability of television to peasants and retired persons. Also, the question was not directly related to functions that the media served for the individual. However, at most educational levels, television was deemed the best source of information for domestic and world politics, followed generally by newspapers and radio. Among peasants, radio was the most significant source of information for both national and international affairs. However, for local news the press was considered most useful for all educational levels (other than peasants), followed by radio and then television.

Asked for preferences between only radio and television, more than two-thirds or more at every level of education said they preferred television. Only the nonprofessional workers at the grade school level were more likely to prefer radio.

As was the case in Belgrade, however, there was no data on decision-making or on media behavior with respect to specific problems, the foci of our study.

Findings

Let us turn now to our own data. The relationships of education of knowledge and decision-making in Ljubljana were similar to those in Belgrade in two respects: amount of knowledge and orientation to solutions. But those of higher education in Ljubljana were not more likely to compare one problem to another, nor did they use distinguishing attributes. Rather, they were more likely to express "self-concern" as an attribute. It was possible that this was due to a special local problem in Ljubljana at the time of our interviewing—a snowstorm that made transportation difficult for many respondents.

Because knowledge and decision-making were similar to data for Belgrade, we expected similar media use and communication. More of those of higher education did use more sources of information, and more used television, press, friends, and references to personal experience. But, possibly because of greater use of radio by the less-educated group in Ljubljana, there was less use of television by this group than in Belgrade. The lesser use of friends by the lower educated group in Ljubljana also was provocative. It suggested more individualized decision-making behavior.

However, interpersonal communication was similar to that observed in Belgrade, and the lower-education group expressed more of an interest in obtaining additional information about local problems. This might imply, as we have suggested, a greater ability to make decisions.

We assumed that there would be fewer differences in media evaluation by educational levels within Ljubljana, consistent with more homogeneity in knowledge, decision-making, media use, and communication. However, more highly education respondents said the press was most useful and fewer tended to find personal experience most useful.

The bases for judging the utility of sources also differed. More of those of the highest education tended to value the media for their content, while more of those of lower education tended to value the media most for their availability—a less discriminating response.

Overall, behavior among educational groupings was similar in Ljubljana to that in Belgrade, with these differences:

- More sophisticated cognitive behaviors across comparable educational levels, very possibly a function of higher income levels in Ljubljana.

- More homogeneity in Ljubljana across educational groupings.
- A much greater use of radio in Ljubljana.

SEATTLE

Background

We faced a problem in presenting prior research on our Seattle variables. A good deal more media research had been done in Belgrade and in Ljubljana, both capital cities of republics, than in Seattle, although it is the largest city in the state of Washington. But since regional differences in media use are not great in the United States, a sampling of media research would be relevant.

A very few studies illustrate the general consistency of relationships of education to media exposure in all three cities.

Viewing of television news was modestly correlated with levels of education in a 1971 national newspaper reading study in the United States. Westley and Severin (1964) found that the group with less than high school education tended most to be nonreaders of newspapers, followed by the high school and some-college group, and then by young college graduates. A study done by Dan E. Clark II and Associates found that, among those with only a high school education, there was a greater tendency to have seen television than to have read the daily newspaper in that community, but this tendency was reversed among those with any college education.

In a report by the Roper Organization, Inc., a 14-year review of studies on what people think of television and other mass media was reported. In November 1972 64 percent of a national sample said they got "most of their news on what's going on in the world today" from television, compared to 50 percent from newspapers. Some persons gave more than one response. Radio was at 21 percent, magazines at 6 percent, and people at 4 percent. Television had increased and newspapers and radio decreased in popularity over this period.

Roper also asked about the relative "credibility" of the media. In this case, television (48 percent) was the medium that people said they would most likely be inclined to believe if there were "conflicting reports," while 21 percent said newspapers, 10 percent magazines, and 8 percent radio.

Finally, Roper asked which of the media the individual would most want to keep, if only one could be kept. In this case 56 percent said television, 22 percent newspapers, 16 percent radio, and 5 percent magazines.

Westley and Severin also asked which of television, radio, or newspapers was most important in finding out about local community events. At that time, the results were favorable to newspapers. Newspapers were also judged more useful for finding out about what is going on, but television was judged most credible. By sociodemographic groupings, professionals, those who had some college, and males preferred newspapers.

Annually since 1966, Opinion Research Corp., has asked a national sample where they would be most likely to find news in which they were interested. Each time those with the highest education are most likely to select newspapers, while those of the lowest education select television. The college-educated group also tended to be more in disagreement with the general point of view of their daily newspaper than the less-educated members of the sample.

Findings

Let us turn now to our data for Seattle. At this point the reader should refer back to our methodological approach, which is different from that utilized by Roper and others. Our data is based upon the use and evaluation of information about a problem that was important to our respondents at a particular time. It is not based on "attitudinal" questions that ask the respondent to judge media usefulness over an extended period of time. Hence, preferences for media and modes of evaluation of media should be quite different in our data.

With respect to knowledge and decision-making, more of those of higher education were able to propose a greater number of problems, to compare problems rather than make references to "self," to give more attributes for problems, and to cite more solutions for those problems. Thus, as in Belgrade and Ljubljana, education was a significant factor in knowledge and decision-making.

Findings for media use and communication also were similar to those observed for Belgrade and Ljubljana. Seattle was more like Ljubljana in its use of radio, which might be a product of the greater availability and different functions of radio. Respondents in Seattle also reported less knowledge of local problems on the basis of personal observation. This could be a product of the physical remoteness of some local problems from individuals in Seattle and the consequent attention given to the problems by media.

A markedly greater number of individuals in Seattle cited media sources. This was most evident for television and the press, although also present for radio.

The greatest differences across communities in reports of media use occurred at the lowest levels of education. This would appear to reflect economic availability factors.

Media evaluation followed the pattern set in Ljubljana. More of those of lower education cited television as the most useful source, while the more highly educated were slightly more likely to mention the press. These findings challenge the Roper data.

The bases for judging the utility of media sources did not vary markedly among educational groupings, although the least educated, as might be expected, cited channel characteristics as their most important criterion. Surprisingly, more of those of higher education tended to cite the availability and trust of sources. These had been demonstrated in other contexts to be less discriminating responses. Possibly the special nature of the local problem—unemployment, with its consequent uncertainty—produced this pattern of responses.

TABLE 8.1

Belgrade: Knowledge and Decision-Making on Local Problems, by Education (percentages)

Variable	Primary	Secondary	University	Significance
Number of local problems				.00*
1	11	4	4	
2	28	21	17	
3+	61	75	79	
Number of local solutions				.00*
1	58	47	38	
2	24	33	33	
3+	18	20	29	
Compares one problem to another	49	56	65	.00*
Attributes for only one problem	13	11	20	.01
Problem is important only to self	39	43	39	n
Reasons why problem is important				.00*
0	15	7	3	
1	65	68	63	
2	20	24	33	
3+	1	1	1	

*Significance equals less than .01.

TABLE 8.2

Belgrade: Media Use and Communication on Local Problems, by Education (percentages)

Variable		Primary	Secondary	University	Significance
Discussed problem		65	80	84	.00*
Attended meeting		25	34	44	.00*
Wanted more information		52	61	59	.05
Number of sources for local problems					.00*
1		35	21	17	
2		19	19	19	
3+		47	60	65	
Mentioned TV		32	39	44	.02
Mentioned radio		24	24	28	n
Mentioned press		38	59	69	.00*
Mentioned friend		28	45	49	.00*
Mentioned family		10	11	15	n
Mentioned personal experience		82	90	91	.00*
Number of source attributes termed most useful	1+	53	70	76	.00*

*Significance equals less than .01.

TABLE 8.3

Belgrade: Media Preference on Local Problems, by Education (percentages)

Media Preference	Primary	Secondary	University
TV	17	16	11
Radio	3	3	1
Press	28	33	45
Friend	7	7	11
Personal experience	45	41	32

Significance equals .10.

TABLE 8.4

Belgrade: Media Evaluation on Local Problems, by Education (percentages)

Why Useful	Primary	Secondary	University
Trust	12	11	10
Availability	50	43	35
Cognitive	19	23	30
Channel	19	23	25

Significance equals n (.2).

TABLE 8.5

Ljubljana: Knowledge and Decision-Making on Local Problems, by Education (percentages)

Variable	Primary	Secondary	University	Significance
Number of local problems				.00*
1	23	10	4	
2	28	20	14	
3+	49	70	82	
Number of local solutions				.00*
1	58	45	34	
2	27	35	32	
3+	15	20	34	
Compares one problem to another	25	32	28	.21
Attributes for only one problem	12	12	15	n
Problem is important only to self	39	46	56	.01
Reasons why problem is important				.00*
0	27	18	7	
1	65	70	79	
2	7	13	13	
3+	1	0	0	

*Significance equals less than .01.

TABLE 8.6

Ljubljana: Media Use and Communication on Local Problems, by Education (percentages)

Variable	Primary	Secondary	University	Significance
Discussed problem	81	87	94	.00*
Attended meeting	23	29	50	.00*
Wanted more information	62	65	58	n
Number of sources for local problems				.03
1	42	33	29	
2	14	14	8	
3+	44	53	63	
Mentioned TV	22	34	39	.00*
Mentioned radio	19	29	37	.00*
Mentioned press	32	49	64	.00*
Mentioned friend	29	36	29	.00*
Mentioned family	8	8	10	n
Mentioned personal experience	78	84	89	.03
Number of source attributes termed most useful 1+	40	55	65	.00*

*Significance equals less than .01.

TABLE 8.7

Ljubljana: Media Preference on Local Problems, by Education (percentages)

Media Preference	Primary	Secondary	University
TV	12	17	11
Radio	1	3	0
Press	39	39	49
Friend	4	7	6
Personal experience	44	34	34

Note: Significance equals n.

TABLE 8.8

Ljubljana: Media Evaluation on Local Problems, by Education (percentages)

Why Useful	Primary	Secondary	University
Trust	14	13	16
Availability	46	41	20
Cognitive	30	38	53
Channel	10	8	11

Note: Significance equals .04.

TABLE 8.9

Seattle: Knowledge and Decision-Making on Local Problems, by Education (percentages)

Variable	Primary	Secondary	University	Significance
Number of local problems				.00*
1	10	4	4	
2	25	16	10	
3+	66	80	86	
Number of local solutions				.00*
0	37	19	11	
1	26	28	27	
2	16	28	29	
3+	20	26	33	
Compares one problem to another	12	16	24	.02
Attributes for only one problem	26	39	41	.03
Problem is important only to self	47	56	54	n
Reasons why problem is important				.02
0	24	12	10	
1	34	35	34	
2	34	36	40	
3+	9	18	16	

*Significance equals less than .01.

TABLE 8.10

Seattle: Media Use and Communication on Local Problems, by Education (percentages)

Variable	Primary	Secondary	University	Significance
Discussed problem	76	86	96	.00*
Attended meeting	23	28	50	.00*
Wanted more information	53	57	50	n
Number of sources for local problems				.00*
0	15	5	3	
1	10	7	4	
2	13	11	10	
3+	62	77	83	
Mentioned TV	52	62	66	.05
Mentioned radio	29	38	45	.03
Mentioned press	55	76	87	.00*
Mentioned friend	41	54	50	.05
Mentioned family	15	19	18	n
Mentioned personal experience	62	63	63	n
Number of source attributes termed most useful				
0	36	18	13	.00*
1	47	60	55	
2+	17	22	32	

*Significance equals less than .01.

TABLE 8.11

Seattle: Media Preference on
Local Problems, by Education
(percentages)

Media Evaluation	Primary	Secondary	University
TV	24	23	16
Radio	4	5	3
Press	38	40	46
Friend	12	13	12
Personal experience	22	19	23

Note: Significance equals n.

TABLE 8.12

Seattle: Media Evaluation on
Local Problems, by Education
(percentages)

Why Useful	Primary	Secondary	University
Trust	2	16	7
Availability	14	26	27
Cognitive	37	32	36
Channel	47	26	30

Note: Significance equals .02.

CHAPTER 9
EDUCATION AND WORLD PROBLEMS

We expected that education would function more dramatically with respect to world problems than for local problems. Because world problems are more abstract, there should be more dependence upon the media, and different processes of decision-making might be at work.

BELGRADE

Those of higher education in Belgrade were appreciably more able to name world problems, provide attributes for those problems, and propose solutions. And the most educated groupings also did more comparing and describing of problems. These were discriminating, content-relevant ways of characterizing problems.

A cultural factor that became apparent was that fewer world problems than local problems were proposed in Belgrade at every educational level. Later it also became apparent that those in Belgrade used more sources of information to deal with fewer world (than local) problems. Relevant to this was less of a tendency to compare one problem to another and was less of a tendency to state that world problems were of personal concern. Thus there was less discrimination and less involvement.

Media use and communication was more marked for world problems. We can surmise that there was less opportunity for the individual to observe world problems and hence there was more media-dependence.

More of those of higher education used multiple sources of information, and there was markedly greater use of media by all educational groupings. The increases in use of radio and television were the most dramatic. Interestingly, the use of friends as sources of information about world problems was much less. Friends were perceived as no more capable of validating world events than the individuals themselves.

We also expected more critical evaluation of media for world problems.

Interestingly, television increased the most in its utility as a source of information for all educational levels. Personal observation, as expected, fell off dramatically. The greater utility of television was reflected in more media evaluations being made on the basis of channel dimensionalities. The factors of sight and sound were more significant for world news.

Finally, across all educational levels there was less interest in having more information. A possible implication was that there was less need for "more information" than for assistance in evaluating the information that the individual had at his disposal.

LJUBLJANA

While greater attention was given to local problems than to world problems in Belgrade, this was not the case in Ljubljana. Nonetheless, similar patterns of knowledge and decision-making held true. Those of higher education named more world problems, gave more reasons for their importance, offered more solutions, and tended more to compare one world problem with another rather than merely stating that it was important to them, personally.

Nonetheless, there were cultural differences. In Belgrade, there was a tendency to propose more solutions for local problems than for world problems. That finding was reversed in Ljubljana.

Media use and communication was similar to that in Belgrade. The high educational levels used more media of every kind and the use of media for world problems was greater than for local problems. But again there were cultural differences. Radio was used significantly more by all educational levels in Ljubljana, a product of the availability of more radio sources.

These differences extended to media evaluation. In Ljubljana those of higher education showed markedly less preference for television accompanied by a greater preference for the press. In evaluation of media, those in Ljubljana were more likely to use content criteria and less likely to employ channel and availability criteria—less discriminating responses.

SEATTLE

But Seattle respondents did less comparing of world problems at each educational level. Rather, they tended to distinguish one world problem from others. Accompanying this was much more of a tendency to express personal involvement in the world problem. This problem obviously was Vietnam. Here again, the nature or importance of the problem appeared to have an effect.

Contrary to what we had observed in Belgrade and Ljubljana, there were few differences in media use and communication as we moved from local to world problems. This appeared to be a function of greater coverage of local news by Seattle television. And there were few differences across educational levels in interpersonal communication and group discussion.

Differences in media evaluation also were not dramatic. More of those of the highest education rated the press most useful, and fewer rated television most useful. Ljubljana, by contrast, was more dependent on television.

Interestingly, however, personal experience was rated as useful by more of those of highest education. In evaluating media, those of the least education tended to use trust slightly more as a criterion; otherwise, there were no differences that could be seen as a function of education. We found this to be of interest.

TABLE 9.1

Belgrade: Knowledge and Decision-Making on World Problems, by Education (percentages)

Variable		Primary	Secondary	University	Significance
Number of world problems					.00*
1		25	17	11	
2		37	33	23	
3+		38	50	66	
Number of world solutions					.10
1		57	52	44	
2		24	31	35	
3+		19	17	21	
Compares one problem to another		38	36	62	.00*
Attributes for only one problem		23	25	24	n
Problem is important only to self		19	18	15	n
Reasons why problem is important	1+	73	87	95	.00*

*Significance equals less than .01.

TABLE 9.2

Belgrade: Media Use and Communication on World Problems, by Education (percentages)

Variable	Primary	Secondary	University	Significance
Discussed problem	57	81	87	.00*
Attended meeting	23	43	55	.00*
Wanted more information	37	47	47	.02
Number of sources for world problems				.00*
1	19	9	7	
2	14	12	11	
3+	67	79	83	
Mentioned TV	51	65	72	.00*
Mentioned radio	40	56	57	.00*
Mentioned press	51	82	89	.00*
Mentioned friend	23	27	33	.04
Mentioned family	10	13	15	.21
Mentioned personal experience	41	37	48	.03
Number of source attributes termed most useful 1+	58	81	89	.00*

*Significance equals less than .01.

TABLE 9.3

Belgrade: Media Preference on World Problems, by Education (percentages)

Media Preference	Primary	Secondary	University
TV	50	39	35
Radio	8	4	2
Press	27	50	57
Friend	2	2	2
Personal experience	13	5	4

Note: Significance equals .00 (less than .01).

TABLE 9.4

Belgrade: Media Evaluation on World Problems, by Education (percentages)

Why Useful	Primary	Secondary	University
Trust	6	11	10
Availability	29	21	23
Cognitive	26	35	30
Channel	39	33	37

Note: Significance equals .10.

TABLE 9.5

Ljubljana: Knowledge and Decision-Making on World Problems, by Education (percentages)

Variable	Primary	Secondary	University	Significance
Number of world problems				.00*
1	16	5	4	
2	30	18	13	
3+	54	77	83	
Number of world solutions				.00*
0	35	21	10	
1	33	31	27	
2	17	25	29	
3+	15	23	34	
Compares one problem to another	16	29	38	.00*
Attributes for only one problem	40	40	43	n
Problem is important only to self	32	38	31	.24
Reasons why problem is important				.09
0	31	19	19	
1	31	27	29	
2	29	37	36	
3+	9	16	17	

*Significance equals less than .01.

TABLE 9.6

Ljubljana: Media Use and Communication on World Problems, by Education (percentages)

Variable	Primary	Secondary	University	Significance
Discussed problem	78	88	95	.00*
Attended meeting	24	38	45	.00*
Wanted more information	44	50	51	n
Number of sources for world problems				.00*
1	23	9	7	
2	9	5	5	
3+	68	86	88	
Mentioned TV	47	74	68	.00*
Mentioned radio	54	68	64	.00*
Mentioned press	61	84	89	.00*
Mentioned friend	27	38	30	.02
Mentioned family	8	15	14	.07
Mentioned personal experience	42	44	54	.07
Number of source attributes termed most useful 1+	55	78	82	.00*

*Significance equals less than .01.

TABLE 9.7

Ljubljana: Media Preference on World Problems, by Education (percentages)

Media Preference	Primary	Secondary	University
TV	38	35	20
Radio	13	9	2
Press	39	50	67
Friend	0	3	3
Personal experience	10	3	8

Note: Significance equals .00 (less than .01).

TABLE 9.8

Ljubljana: Media Evaluation on World Problems, by Education (percentages)

Why Useful	Primary	Secondary	University
Trust	10	8	9
Availability	39	35	27
Cognitive	27	38	54
Channel	24	19	10

Note: Significance equals .02.

TABLE 9.9

Seattle: Knowledge and Decision-Making on World Problems, by Education (percentages)

Variable	Primary	Secondary	University	Significance
Number of world problems				.00*
1	16	5	4	
2	30	18	13	
3+	54	77	83	
Number of world solutions				.00*
0	35	21	10	
1	33	31	27	
2	17	25	29	
3+	15	23	34	
Compares one problem to another	16	29	38	.00*
Attributes for only one problem	40	40	43	n
Problem is important only to self	32	38	31	.24
Reasons why problem is important				.09
0	31	19	19	
1	31	27	29	
2	29	37	36	
3+	9	16	17	

*Significance equals less than .01.

TABLE 9.10

Seattle: Media Use and Communication on World Problems, by Education (percentages)

Variable	Primary	Secondary	University	Significance
Discussed problem	77	85	91	.01
Attended meeting	25	35	45	.01
Wanted more information	44	50	52	n
Number of sources for world problems				.00*
0	16	7	4	
1	9	5	4	
2	16	9	12	
3+	59	79	80	
Mentioned TV	56	72	69	.01
Mentioned radio	35	48	45	.05
Mentioned press	60	80	83	.00*
Mentioned friend	36	45	39	.17
Mentioned family	16	18	17	n
Mentioned personal experience	38	48	51	.10
Number of source attributes termed most useful				.02
0	26	18	15	
1	58	62	57	
2+	16	21	29	

*Significance equals less than .01.

TABLE 9.11

Seattle: Media Preference on World Problems, by Education (percentages)

Media Preference	Primary	Secondary	University
TV	39	33	26
Radio	4	2	0
Press	39	44	54
Friend	9	7	3
Personal experience	9	14	17

Note: Significance equals .08.

TABLE 9.12

Seattle: Media Evaluation on World Problems, by Education (percentages)

Why Useful	Primary	Secondary	University
Trust	14	8	7
Availability	24	25	23
Cognitive	35	38	36
Channel	27	29	34

Note: Significance equals n.

CHAPTER

10

SEX ROLE AND LOCAL PROBLEMS

The distinctions between male and female roles have been illustrated in a number of Yugoslav media studies. Almost all have shown a preference for the press by men, while women preferred radio, and later, television.

Bacević (1965a) showed that males were more often readers of newspapers. Bacević (1965b) also found that men were heavier users of all media. This finding was confirmed by Danojlić (1965a), who reported that males much more preferred informational and political columns and (1965b) also more preferred "news content."

Bacević (1965c) found that men were three times as likely to be better informed. Leandrov (1967) asked which media respondents would be least willing to give up. Men and women had similar values for the press, but women were less willing to give up television and men were less willing to give up radio. Asked about discussion at meetings, men were much more likely to say that they participated in the discussion (Dimković, 1967).

BELGRADE

In our data, Belgrade was the culture with the most highly differentiated male-female roles. Thus it was expected that men would be able to name significantly more local problems, suggest more solutions for those problems, and compare problems in formulating solutions. However, women were as able as men to describe why a local problem was important. The reason was because it affected them personally.

Thus, while men were aware of a greater range of local problems, affecting more persons, and were more attuned to proposing solutions for those problems, women saw the importance of local problems in personal terms. Women faced these problems, but the solutions did not lie in their hands as often.

Men also engaged in more media use and communication relevant to these decisions.

Men more than women cited a greater number of sources of information and reported more use of television, radio, and substantially more use of the press. Interestingly, Belgrade men, more than women, discussed local problems with other persons. The work role of men also permitted more discussion of local problems at meetings.

The female sex role expressed itself in other ways. Women reported as much contact with friends, more discussion with members of the family, and as much direct contact with the problems—i.e., learning by personal experience. Almost as much as men, women wanted additional information about the local problems.

In media evaluation, more men cited the press as their "most useful" sources of information, while more women cited personal experience.

The reasons for the judgments were more revealing of differences in male-female roles. More women tended to cite the availability of media while more men gave content and channel reasons. Thus discriminations by men were more sophisticated.

LJUBLJANA

We expected fewer differences in media use and communication consistent with less differentiated sex roles in Ljubljana.

Earlier research in Slovenia and Ljubljana was supportive of these expectations. As examples, Radio 1967 by the Institute of Sociology showed that women of the lowest education listened appreciably more to radio than did men of lower education, but radio listening of men and women was similar at higher levels of education.

Television 1967 by Kroflic et al. said women were significantly less likely than men to watch television news, less likely to watch regularly, or to assert that news was their favorite show.

Asked in Slovenia 1969 by Vreg about the medium of communication they would least be willing to give up, women were slightly more attracted to radio and men slightly more to newspapers, with no difference in preferences for television.

With respect to readership of daily newspapers in Ljubljana, more men than women read Delo, while there were no differences in readership of Dnevnik or Vecer.

Asked about content preferences, males more than females read about world and national politics but not more about local news.

These studies showed mixed results. We expected that our variables, in situational settings, would give us a better idea of the locus of male-female differences if they existed.

With respect to knowledge and decision-making, men in Ljubljana did not demonstrate a great degree of discrepancy from the behavior of women. More men were able to name local problems, but not significantly so, and to provide more solutions, but again the differences were less discrepant than in Belgrade.

Men and women in Ljubljana were not different in their tendencies to compare local problems or to see local problems as important to themselves, personally. Men did not cite significantly more reasons for the importance of the problems than did women, indicating that in Ljubljana the local problems were as important to men as to women. Again, the results were mixed.

Because of the lack of discrepancies, we expected few differences in media use and communication. Our expectations were confirmed in almost every respect. Men and women cited approximately the same number of media sources. Within media, men and women used television and radio similarly. Men used the press more than women, but the discrepancy was not great. Men and women cited friendships, referred to family contacts, and cited personal experience equally. They also equally were engaged in discussions with other persons, and they expressed similar desires for information.

The male-female role discrepancy was clearly expressed only in discussions carried out at meetings, to which women obviously had less access.

There were somewhat surprising differences, however, in media evaluation. Males more than females cited television, a less discriminating medium, as most useful. However, men cited content criteria as the bases for valuing television, while women cited availability, a less discriminating response. Thus the male role asserted itself more subtly.

SEATTLE

A national news study published in 1971 by the American Newspaper Publishers Association, a comparable base period for our study, showed that men read more foreign and national news while women read more human interest reports. Among the least read items by women were political columns and education news. Women were no more likely than men to agree with the point of view of their newspaper, and there were no differences in their tendency to be critical of their newspaper.

A study in the small community of Salem, Oregon, showed that, with respect to a particular story, in most cases men tended to have read it in the newspaper while women tended more to have seen it on television or heard it on the radio.

In our own data, the situational nature of the research provided a fresh test of hypothesized differences between men's and women's roles.

As an example, we found that women, somewhat more than men, were more able to name local problems. But they were somewhat less able to suggest solutions for those problems, although they were as able as men to compare and to describe them. There was an expected tendency on the part of Seattle men and women to observe that the local problem—unemployment—was important to them personally. This problem not only affected those individuals who lost jobs but also brought about an awareness of what was happening to others.

Because of the lack of discrepancies with respect to knowledge and decision-making, we expected few differences between men and women in media use and communication. As hypothesized, men did not differ from women in the number of media sources they had used. Nor were there differences in the use of radio, newspapers, friends, interpersonal discussion, discussion at meetings, or in seeking information. However, there was greater use by women of television and the family as sources of information.

More women named television as their most useful as well as their most used source, but more men cited the press. The overall pattern was more similar to Ljubljana than to Belgrade.

Criteria used for judging media were consistent with the nature of the preferences. More men gave content reasons for finding their sources of information more useful, while more women cited channel dimensionalities. This was associated with women's preferences for television.

Since education had proved such a strong predictor, we examined education in relation to sex roles: Did men and women of equivalent education behave similarly or differently? To the extent that they behaved differently, we might attribute those differences to sex role. If they behaved similarly, we could attribute that to the effects of education.

We expected sex roles to retain more strength in Belgrade even though differences should be reduced by the effects of education. As we expected, when men and women in Belgrade were compared at equivalent levels of education, differences remained that might properly be attributed to sex roles. Women of equivalent education proposed fewer solutions for local problems and used less complex problem-solving techniques than men; i.e, there was more of a tendency to use self rather than more discriminating attributes as a basis for evaluating local problems.

Women also used media less, usually the print media, but this varied by levels of education. And women discussed local problems less, particularly in meetings. Also, the family was a more useful source of information for women with the exception of women of university education, who did not use the family more as a source of communication than did men at the same educational level.

In Ljubljana, we expected the male-female differences to be more affected by education. This turned out to be the case. There were only scattered sex-role discrepancies, most of them at the university level of education: For example, men proposed more reasons why problems were important, and men also did more comparing of local problems. Further, women used more radio and television, an expected corollary of more restricted cognitive behavior. And men discussed problems more at meetings.

Otherwise, almost all other differences were eliminated.

In Seattle, sex-role differences were largely eliminated by education. Men tended to express somewhat more knowledge and decision-making, but the male-female differences in Seattle occurred primarily at the lowest level of education. Seattle's blue-collar, low-education group actually was as extreme in male-female sex roles as in Belgrade, a rather provocative finding.

At the lowest educational level, women were somewhat more knowledgeable, although less engaged in decision-making. This is a crucial distinction. Men used more sources of information, notably radio and newspapers, and engaged in more discussion.

Women of the highest education tended to use the most sources of information, suggesting a "working harder" hypothesis; that is, women who engaged in decision-making apparently felt a need to fortify it with more information than did men. Nonetheless, women continued to use and prefer television and the family as sources of information, which are suggestive of female social roles. Men tended more to cite personal experience.

Television, to judge by these preferences, appeared to be more effective for women as a source of information than for solving problems. It would be interesting to learn why women found more information in television than men did. Perhaps the nature of the problems, as women defined them, were different.

TABLE 10.1

Belgrade: Knowledge and Decision-Making on Local Problems, by Sex (percentages)

Variable	Male	Female	Significance
Number of local problems			.00*
1	5	8	
2	18	25	
3+	77	67	
Number of local solutions			.00*
0	1	1	
1	41	54	
2	32	28	
3+	26	17	
Compares one problem to another	65	55	.00*
Attribute for only one problem	16	14	n
Problem is important only to self	36	50	.00*
Reasons why problem is important			
0	2	3	n
1	71	69	
2	26	26	
3+	1	1	

*Significance equals less than .01.

TABLE 10.2

Belgrade: Media Use and Communication on Local Problems, by Sex (percentages)

Variable	Male	Female	Significance
Discussed problem	83	71	.00*
Attended meeting	47	23	.00*
Wanted more information.	60	56	.15
Number of sources for local problems			.01
0	3	3	
1	19	28	
2	18	19	
3+	60	50	.01
Mentioned TV	44	38	.09
Mentioned radio	30	23	.02
Mentioned press	67	49	.00*
Mentioned friend	44	43	n
Mentioned family	8	15	.00*
Mentioned personal experience	94	93	n
Number of source attributes termed most useful			.02
0	28	32	
1	55	56	
2+	17	11	

*Significance equals less than .01.

TABLE 10.3

Belgrade: Media Preference on Local Problems, by Sex
(percentages)

Media Preference	Male	Female
TV	16	16
Radio	3	2
Press	39	30
Friend	6	10
Personal experience	36	42

Note: Significance equals .10.

TABLE 10.4

Belgrade: Media Evaluation on Local
Problems, by Sex
(percentages)

Why Useful	Male	Female
Trust	10	13
Availability	36	48
Cognitive	28	20
Channel	26	19

Note: Significance equals .01.

TABLE 10.5

Ljubljana: Knowledge and Decision-Making on Local Problems, by Sex (percentages)

Variable	Male	Female	Significance
Number of local problems			.18
1	13	11	
2	17	23	
3+	70	54	
Number of local solutions			.02
0	4	7	
1	39	47	
2	34	27	
3+	23	19	
Compares one problem to another	34	31	n
Attribute for only one problem	14	14	n
Problem is important only to self	49	51	n
Reasons why problem is important			n
0	10	11	
1	77	77	
2	12	12	
3+	1	0	

TABLE 10.6

Ljubljana: Media Use and Communication in Local Problems, by Sex
(percentages)

Variable	Male	Female	Significance
Discussed problem	88	87	n
Attended meeting	38	26	.00*
Wanted more information	64	62	n
Number of sources for local problems			n
0	1	2	
1	35	34	
2	13	12	
3+	1	0	
Mentioned TV	35	37	n
Mentioned radio	31	30	n
Mentioned press	56	48	.05
Mentioned friend	34	38	n
Mentioned family	8	11	n
Mentioned personal experience	91	92	n
Number of source attributes termed most useful			.21
0	42	42	
1	42	46	
2+	16	12	

*Significance equals less than .01.

TABLE 10.7

Ljubljana: Media Preference on Local Problems, by Sex (percentages)

Media Preference	Male	Female
TV	19	11
Radio	2	1
Press	41	41
Friend	9	4
Personal experience	29	43

Note: Significance equals .01.

TABLE 10.8

Ljubljana: Media Evaluation on Local Problems, by Sex (percentages)

Why Useful	Male	Female
Trust	14	14
Availability	32	42
Cognitive	44	36
Channel	10	8

Note: Significance equals n.

TABLE 10.9

Seattle: Knowledge and Decision-Making on Local Problems, by Sex (percentages)

Variable	Male	Female	Significance
Number of local problems			.11
1	6	4	
2	18	13	
3+	76	83	
Number of local solutions			.06
0	12	19	
1	30	28	
2	27	28	
3+	31	25	
Compares one problem to another	20	17	n
Attribute for only one problem	36	42	.19
Problem is important only to self	56	58	n
Reasons why problem is important			.08
0	12	6	
1	34	37	
2	37	41	
3+	17	16	

TABLE 10.10

Seattle: Media Use and Communication on Local Problems, by Sex (percentages)

Variable	Male	Female	Significance
Discussed problem	86	89	n
Attended meeting	33	33	n
Wanted more information	53	57	n
Number of sources for local problems			n
0	1	1	
1	7	7	
2	14	9	
3+	78	83	
Mentioned TV	60	70	.02
Mentioned radio	42	40	n
Mentioned press	80	79	n
Mentioned friend	52	55	n
Mentioned family	13	26	.00*
Mentioned personal experience	70	62	.04
Number of source attributes termed most useful			.10
0	14	16	
1	57	62	
2+	29	22	

*Significance equals less than .01

TABLE 10.11

Seattle: Media Preference on Local Problems, by Sex (percentages)

Media Preference	Male	Female
TV	17	26
Radio	5	4
Press	45	37
Friend	11	14
Personal experience	22	19

Note: Significance equals less than .10.

TABLE 10.12

Seattle: Media Evaluation on Local Problems, by Sex (percentages)

Why Useful	Male	Female
Trust	10	13
Availability	23	25
Cognitive	40	28
Channel	27	34

Note: Significance equals less than .10.

CHAPTER

11

SEX ROLE AND WORLD PROBLEMS

We speculated that differences in sex roles would be most expressed with regard to world problems, for world problems are more remote from the individual and require a greater background of experience. Local problems could be more easily coped with as a part of one's everyday activities. Crossculturally, we again expected to observe more discrepancies between male and female roles in Belgrade than in Ljubljana and Seattle.

BELGRADE

As we had expected, there were more dramatic differences between men and women in Belgrade in terms of knowledge and decision-making about world problems. Men named more world problems and proposed more solutions for those problems, and more men compared one problem to another as a way of describing the problems.

Although women concerned themselves with fewer world problems, they learned more about them. Yet women were less able to propose solutions. This would be consistent in Belgrade with to the sex role.

If the essential differences between male and female roles were in decision-making rather than in knowledge about problems, variations in media use and evaluation might not follow a regular pattern. Thus men used more sources of information only slightly more than women, and there were no differences in use of television, friends, or even in personal experience with world problems. However, men used radio and the press appreciably more than women did. Thus although that decision-making was primarily a male role in Belgrade, women were almost as well informed and used media (other than press and radio) to much the same extent.

Media evaluation should be expressive of patterns in knowledge and decision-making. Reflecting this, more women cited again television as the most useful source of information, while more men rated the press as most useful. But there were no differences in the criteria used for the evaluation of media. Men and women equally cited content characteristics.

LJUBLJANA

In Ljubljana, we expected that there would be fewer differences based upon sex roles. This hypothesis appeared to be tenable with regard to knowledge and decision-making. Men did not, any more than women in Ljubljana, tend to name more problems, more reasons for the importance of problems, or more solutions to problems.

The substantial differences were in the greater tendency for men to compare one problem to another, while women in Ljubljana were more likely to perceive world problems as being important to themselves, personally. This, too, was a provocative finding with respect to role. It suggested that women were more able to project and to identify themselves with more remote problems and to perceive them in personal terms.

We did not expect, therefore, any great differences in media use and evaluation. Women and men employed the same number of sources of information, and within media there were no differences with respect to television, radio, press, friendships, or personal experience. The only difference between men and women was in the tendency for more women to cite the family as a source of information.

Nonetheless, there were implications for media evaluation. Not unexpectedly, somewhat more women, but fewer than in Belgrade, rated television as their most useful source, while men cited the press as most useful (here again, the discrepancies were not as great as in Belgrade). However, there were once more significant differences between men and women in the criteria used for evaluating media. More women cited availability of media as a reason for usefulness, while more men cited content characteristics.

SEATTLE

Men and women in Seattle named a similar number of world problems and cited a similar number of reasons for the importance of those problems. Men were somewhat more able than women, to propose solutions for world problems. And men tended slightly more to compare one problem with another, while women again tended to perceive world problems in personal terms. The results were similar to what we had observed in Ljubljana and especially Belgrade.

Men and women did not differ, however in the number of sources of information used. Within media, there were no differences in use of radio, press, and discussion, or in the desire for information. However, women were more likely to cite television, friendships, and the family as sources of information. And men were more likely to cite personal experience, doubtlessly a product of wartime experiences.

The most distinctive differences in media evaluation appeared with respect to television. Again, more women than men rated it as most useful. More men rated personal experience as most useful, possibly a function of a broader identification with war.

With respect to the criteria used to judge the utility of content, more women again employed availability as a criterion, and more men cited content criteria.

EDUCATION AND SEX ROLES

When education was equivalent, women were as active as men in comparing problems and in describing the nature of those problems. At the secondary and university levels of education, women mentioned more sources of information—primarily television, the family, and personal experiences. Men at higher levels of education engaged more in discussion at meetings. At the university level of education, men engaged more in interpersonal discussion. These advantages could be attributed to the places in which men found themselves by the nature of their work roles.

In Seattle, educational equivalence greatly reduced most male-female distinctions and eliminated some. The differences that persisted were seen largely in the location of men and women in occupational and family roles and in the tendency for the men to be more accustomed to decision-making and discussion about local and world problems.

TABLE 11.1

Belgrade: Knowledge and Decision-Making on World Problems, by Sex (percentages)

Variable	Male	Female	Significance
Number of world problems			.01
1	15	21	
2	30	34	
3+	55	45	
Number of world solutions			.00*
0	2	1	
1	44	56	
2	35	24	
3+	19	18	
Compares one problem to another	64	54	.01
Attribute for only one problem	24	30	.05
Problem is important only to self	16	24	.00*
Reasons why problem is important			.09
0	5	6	
1	73	66	
2	22	27	
3+	0	1	

*Significance equals less than .01.

TABLE 11.2

Belgrade: Media Use and Communication on World Problems, by Sex (percentages)

Variable	Male	Female	Significance
Discussed problem	84	69	.00*
Attended meeting	55	27	.00*
Wanted more information	44	44	n
Number of sources for world problems			.14
0	2	3	
1	10	12	
2	10	14	
3+	78	71	
Mentioned TV	68	71	.22
Mentioned radio	62	54	.02
Mentioned press	89	78	.00*
Mentioned friend	29	32	n
Mentioned family	11	17	.03
Mentioned personal experience	44	46	n
Number of source attributes termed most useful			n
0	13	16	
1	62	63	
2+	25	21	

*Significance equals less than .01.

TABLE 11.3

Belgrade: Media Preference on
World Problems, by Sex
(percentages)

Media Preference	Male	Female
TV	35	47
Radio	5	5
Press	53	38
Friend	1	2
Personal experience	6	8

Note: Significance equals .00 (less than .01).

TABLE 11.4

Belgrade: Media Evaluation on
World Problems, by Sex
(percentages)

Why Useful	Male	Female
Trust	11	8
Availability	23	23
Cognitive	32	31
Channel	34	38

Note: Significance equals n.

TABLE 11.5

Ljubljana: Knowledge and Decision-Making on World Problems, by Sex (percentages)

Variable	Male	Female	Significance
Number of world problems			n
1	13	12	
2	23	26	
3+	64	62	
Number of world solutions			n
0	7	9	
1	37	40	
2	32	27	
3+	25	24	
Compares one problem to another	52	45	.07
Attribute for only one problem	19	18	n
Problem is important only to self	18	32	.00*
Reasons why problem is important			n
0	13	11	
1	72	70	
2	15	18	
3+	0	1	

*Significance equals less than .01.

TABLE 11.6

Ljubljana: Media Use and Communication on World Problems, by Sex (percentages)

Variable	Male	Female	Significance
Discussed problem	88	86	.23
Attended meeting	44	29	.00*
Wanted more information	53	44	.04
Number of sources for world problems			n
0	2	2	
1	13	9	
2	5	7	
3+	0	1	
Mentioned TV	70	74	.24
Mentioned radio	70	71	n
Mentioned press	86	88	n
Mentioned friend	38	36	n
Mentioned family	11	17	.03
Mentioned personal experience	47	52	.18
Number of source attributes termed most useful			.09
0	23	17	
1	55	62	
2+	22	21	

*Significance equals less than .01.

TABLE 11.7

Ljubljana: Media Preference on World Problems, by Sex (percentages)

Media Preference	Male	Female
TV	31	36
Radio	6	10
Press	56	46
Friend	2	2
Personal experience	5	6

Note: Significance equals .20.

TABLE 11.8

Ljubljana: Media Evaluation on World Problems, by Sex (percentages)

Why Useful	Male	Female
Trust	11	7
Availability	27	41
Cognitive	43	35
Channel	19	17

Note: Significance equals .01.

TABLE 11.9

Seattle: Knowledge and Decision-Making on World Problems, by Sex (percentages)

Variable	Male	Female	Significance
Number of world problems			n
1	7	6	
2	19	19	
3+	75	75	
Number of world solutions			.02
0	12	21	
1	33	31	
2	29	23	
3+	26	25	
Compares one problem to another	34	27	.11
Attribute for only one problem	44	43	n
Problem is important only to self	34	40	.10
Reasons why problem is important			n
0	16	19	
1	31	38	
2	38	36	
3+	15	17	

TABLE 11.10

Seattle: Media Use and Communication on World Problems, by Sex (percentages)

Variable	Male	Female	Significance
Discussed problem	88	77	.13
Attended meeting	38	34	n
Wanted more information	50	50	n
Number of sources for world problems			n
0	4	3	
1	7	5	
2	12	11	
3+	77	81	
Mentioned TV	67	76	.02
Mentioned radio	46	48	n
Mentioned press	79	83	
Mentioned friend	40	48	.05
Mentioned family	14	22	.01
Mentioned personal experience	54	44	.02
Number of source attributes termed most useful			n
0	14	16	
1	64	61	
2+	22	23	

TABLE 11.11

Seattle: Media Preference on World Problems, by Sex (percentages)

Media Preference	Male	Female
TV	26	38
Radio	2	3
Press	47	44
Friend	6	6
Personal experience	19	9

Note: Significance equals .00 (less than .01).

TABLE 11.12

Seattle: Media Evaluation on World Problems, by Sex (percentages)

Why Useful	Male	Female
Trust	10	7
Availability	20	30
Cognitive	40	34
Channel	30	29

Note: Significance equals .20.

CHAPTER

12

AGE ROLE AND LOCAL PROBLEMS

Three age groupings were conceptualized.

First was what we called the early-career group. This was the age group of the twenties. Many of these young people were at the university or were only recently introduced to a job or career.

The second group—the mid-career persons—incorporated the age group of the thirties through the fifties. These persons were established in jobs and professions and in the local and broader community.

Our third group included the post-career persons—those in the age group of the sixties and older. These persons were reducing their participation in jobs and careers in preparation for retirement or a semiactive status.

EARLIER YUGOSLAV STUDIES

Yugoslav studies have produced a variety of definitions of age roles. In nine studies examined by the authors, there was no exact correspondence of age groupings, although there were some similarities. Statistical grouping rather than role conceptualization was the criterion for establishing the boundaries of groups. This has its counterpart in American mass communication research.

One Yugoslav study used ten age groupings, although the most usual number of groupings was four or five. In most studies, the youngest age groupings were cut off at ages varying from 18 to 30. The reasons for these age distributions were seldom stated conceptually.

Intervals within age role categories also varied greatly across studies. Intervals were as small as three to six years. Older groupings began anywhere from age 56 to 66. Middle-age categories ranged in breadth from 5 to 28 years, indicating the difficulties we experienced in comparing the media behavior of age groupings from one study to another.

The age variable also dramatized the danger of comparing research done at different times. Different age groupings make choices among different media (for example, television versus non-television generation), particularly in Yugoslavia, where media availabilities expanded rapidly over the 1966-71 period that our research covers.

Nonetheless, a number of studies conducted in Belgrade provided some indication of how age roles had functioned there with respect to media.

BELGRADE

Background

Summarizing the studies by Bacević, Danojlic, and others, the youngest groupings in Belgrade expressed somewhat less preference for information columns, less preferred radio and television for information content, and saw less utility for the press and radio than did older age groups. They also were least represented at meetings and least informed on news other than foreign affairs.

Contrarily, these studies showed that the youngest age groups were best informed on foreign affairs, were more informed and discriminating in use of all media, tended to read more periodicals, and were most attuned to radio as a source of information and entertainment.

These findings appeared contradictory. The reasons, we surmised, were that the studies were conducted at different times; had differently conceptualized age groups; and were ambiguous as to the nature of the content of the media with which they were concerned.

The behavior of the mid-career group appeared to be more internally consistent. As compared to the youngest age group, the middle group showed a slight tendency (with the older group) to prefer information columns. Like the youngest age grouping, they tended to be more regular listeners to and users of radio. They also more preferred television for its news content.

The middle career group also was much more present and likely to engage in discussion at meetings, was least willing to give up television among media, and was the most active audience for radio news.

The members of the oldest group demonstrated only a slight tendency, along with middle age groupings, to prefer information columns in the press, but they reported more print readership. They were the least regular listeners to and users of radio, and they less preferred television for news content than did the middle age groupings. With the middle age group, they expressed more utility for press and radio than did the youngest age group. Also, they were more likely to use all media as sources of information.

Nonetheless, those in the oldest group were both the best and poorest informed, made the fewest demands for information, and were less regularly present at meetings than the middle age group.

The oldest age group was thus more attuned to media but at the same time less informed. We hoped that our data, with its situational focus and its articulation of cognitive and communication variables, would clarify these inconsistencies.

Findings

With respect to knowledge and decision-making, it was evident that the mid-career group in Belgrade was more knowledgeable and able to cope with decision-making about local problems. This would be in keeping with their greater involvement in their professions and community.

More members of the mid-career age groups were able to name more local problems, were knowledgeable about problems, and were able to give more sophisticated evaluations of those problems. However, the youngest group was most able to suggest solutions to problems. And in each case the younger group was more comparable to the mid-career group than to the oldest group.

By contrast, the post-career group named the fewest problems, was least knowledgeable about them, gave the least sophisticated evaluations, and was least able to provide solutions. This is a far more consistent portrait than represented in the earlier research. It portrayed more active pre- and mid-career groups and a much less involved and active post-career group.

Given the data on knowledge and decision-making, we could expect the mid-career and younger age groups to engage in more media use and communication. In fact, more of the two younger groupings did utilize multiple sources of information, including television, press, friendships, and personal experience. These groups also engaged in interpersonal communication and wanted more information.

While the mid-career group reported more problems, was more knowledgeable, and was engaged in more complex evaluation of problems, the youngest group was more attuned to media, friendships, and interpersonal communication. It also appeared to be more responsive to new information. This suggested a distinctly different style or age role for each group, in which the youngest group was more attuned to people and information.

The post-career age group was more isolated not only from problems and their solutions but also from the mass media and other persons. More members of the oldest age group reported significantly less use of multiple sources of information, including the press, television, and friends. The last is a particularly telling finding. Overall, we were again able to sketch a far more consistent portrait than was reflected in the earlier Yugoslav research.

Turning to media evaluation, personal experience was most useful to the older groupings, followed by press and television, while more of the younger persons said the press was most useful. Thus, the youngest group was more media dependent and also had greater interpersonal activity.

Differences in style also occurred with respect to the criteria by which media were evaluated. More of the older persons cited availability as a reason for media utility, a non-content relevant criterion, while the younger and mid-career persons employed more content criteria.

LJUBLJANA

Background

Because of what we observed earlier in educational and sex roles in Ljubljana, we looked for more homogeneous age roles as well. The Vreg's Slovenia 1967, for example, showed that there were no differences across age groups in time spent listening to radio. The 1967 study of television in Slovenia found that those up to 50 years of age were more likely to own a television set than those over 50, while those over 60 were least likely to own a set. Older persons in Slovenia also were less interested in TV programs.

Asked about the medium of communication they would be least willing to give up, older persons in Ljubljana preferred radio more than younger persons did, while there were few differences in regard to television and newspapers. However, television preferences appeared to be based more on entertainment, while newspaper preferences were more oriented to public affairs. Younger people were more likely to read each of the three daily newspapers in Ljubljana.

Findings

Knowledge and decision-making in Ljubljana were similar across age groupings to what we had observed in Belgrade. More of the early and mid-career groups named more problems, gave reasons for the importance of problems, and suggested solutions for problems.

But, contrary to our findings for Belgrade, the older groups in Ljubljana provided sophisticated descriptions of problems. The reasons for this might lie in the higher educational levels of the oldest group in Ljubljana as compared to Belgrade. Given this, the pattern was otherwise consistent and predictable.

The young career group engaged in somewhat more media use than the mid-career group and considerably more than the oldest group. More of the early and mid-career groups named multiple sources of information, citing television, the press, friendships, and more of an interest in information.

However, there were no differences in the use of radio, references to family, interpersonal communication, and discussion at meetings. These behaviors were more similar than in Belgrade across age levels, reflecting greater homogeneity in the Ljubljana sample.

More of the oldest group were likely to cite personal experience as their most useful source of information. They appeared in this way to be functioning on the basis of prior rather than present knowledge.

Otherwise, there were few differences in media preferences. All groups rated the press as most useful and used similar criteria to evaluate the utility of sources of information. Media evaluation was more sophisticated, as well as more homogeneous, across age groupings in Ljubljana as compared to Belgrade.

SEATTLE

Background

A national news study carried out in June 1971, a comparable base period for our study, showed that there were few significant patterns of differences among age groups in their preferred reading except that the 25-to-34 age group was more involved than the 18-to-24 age group with news about career-type concerns, while the 18-to-24 age group was somewhat more likely to disagree with the general editorial viewpoint of their newspaper, particularly on national issues.

Westley and Severin (1964b) found that most nonreaders of newspapers were in the age group of the seventies and above, but that those in the next group were in their twenties.

The strongest association of television news viewing with social characteristics in the 1971 national newspaper reading study was represented in age groupings. Some 62 percent of those 65 or older reported watching television news, compared with only 42 percent in the 18-to-24 age category.

Findings

Our data on knowledge and decision-making showed that more of the early and mid-career age groups gave more reasons for the importance of problems, but they did not name more problems and they were not consistently more sophisticated in their evaluation of problems.

However, the younger groups were able to provide more solutions to problems, which could be their most distinguishing characteristic.

More of the two younger career groups also, cite more sources of information, refer more to personal experience, discuss problems at meetings, and express a need for information. But there were no differences across age groupings with respect to the number of sources of information. Nor were there differences with respect to the specific use of television, radio, press, family, and interpersonal communication.

More members of the older age group cited the press as most useful. And, in contrast to Belgrade and Ljubljana, more members of the younger groups tended to cite personal experience, indicating possible situational influences at work in Seattle.

Interestingly, all age groups in Seattle cited television as more useful for local news than had been the case in Belgrade or Ljubljana, while fewer cited personal experience.

There were no significant differences across age groupings in Seattle in the criteria used to evaluate media. Overall, the greatest discrepancies by age groups appeared in Belgrade, while the greatest homogeneity existed in Ljubljana. There appeared to be more differences within each culture with respect to knowledge, decision-making, media use, and communication than there were differences in equivalent groupings across cultures.

AGE AND EDUCATION

By comparing age groups of equivalent levels of education we were able to isolate the effects of age roles as contrasted to the effects of education. We reasoned as follows:

1. The youngest people should be thinking, reading, listening, and discussing problems more because of their age—an activity hypothesis.

2. The mid-career group should be more involved in roles that required problem-solving—a positional hypothesis.

3. But education could extend the live of the older groupings. Otherwise, we would opt for an inactivity hypothesis.

Let us look first at Belgrade. At the primary level of education there remained a significant difference in knowledge and decision-making among the three age groupings. The mid-career group was somewhat more active than the youngest group, and both were more active than the oldest group. Thus a positional role appeared to assert itself with respect to knowledge and decision-making.

A somewhat similar pattern existed at the secondary school level, but the youngest age group in this case was somewhat more knowledgeable than the middle group; i.e., an activity factor.

At the university level of education, differences were greatly reduced. The older, highly educated persons were just as able to name problems (although less able to suggest solutions) and were no less able to provide comparison attributes than the younger people. Age differences were greatly reduced by the continuing effects of education. Inactivity was deferred by education.

Young persons were more exposed to television, press, and friends at the primary level of education, activity thus accounting for differences in behavior. The same pattern existed at the secondary level of education. Expected differences again were mitigated at the highest level of education: Older persons of university education used as many media as younger persons of the same education. Education again postponed inactivity.

The pattern was maintained with respect to media evaluation. Younger persons at both the primary and secondary levels were more able than the oldest persons to evaluate their media sources as useful or not useful. At the primary and secondary levels, the younger groups also were more likely to discuss local problems with others and to want more information about those problems. Thus activity played a role.

Education, once again, functioned for older persons at the university level of education. They were as likely as younger groups to engage in discussion with others, although they were somewhat less likely to want more information.

In Ljubljana there had been factors that caused us to expect fewer differences among the age groupings, given equal education. This appeared to be the case with respect to local problems.

There were no differences in knowledge and decision-making among the age groups with respect to number of problems, but in

Ljubljana, as distinct from Belgrade, young people had more solutions for problems. In Belgrade, young people had named and described more problems. Possibly the young people of Belgrade faced more complex problems that were less susceptible to solutions.

There was a tendency for younger persons, at primary and secondary levels of education, to propose more attributes for the importance of local problems, an activity finding.

There were fewer distinctions in media use and communication; differences existed only at the primary level of education, whereas in Belgrade this had been true at the university level as well. Thus age was a more compelling variable in Belgrade than in Ljubljana. Our cultural context suggested this finding.

As in Belgrade, local problems appeared to be more the province of the young. They reported personal experience as a significantly greater source of information, accompanied by more references to friends. In addition, there was a tendency, at all educational levels, for younger people to say that they wanted more information, again an activity finding.

In Seattle we observed no significant differences in knowledge and decision-making among age groups in describing local problems. Any "age" differences were explained by education.

There were tendencies for younger persons to entertain more solutions at the primary level of education, but not at the university level. By contrast, more of those over 60 years of age at the highest level of education tended to propose solutions to problems.

This reversal in Seattle could be a function of the current youth culture, which at the time was more concerned with pointing out problems than in proposing solutions.

The pattern of media use and communication also was somewhat different in Seattle. Older people at primary levels of education were most dependent on television. Among those of college education, the mid-career age group tended to use television more. This is a provocative finding. It is possible that two different kinds of television exposure were involved. The primary-grade elderly may use television as their only source of local news, while the university mid-career group may use television as a complementary source of information.

There was a significant tendency for older persons to use the press more, at both primary and secondary levels of education. There were no differences at the university level, again demonstrating the importance of a higher education in extending age roles.

There also were no differences in media evaluation. Here the earlier observed differences in age roles can be attributed largely to education.

The most consistent, if not the strongest, differences in age roles occurred in interpersonal communication, discussion at meetings, and desire for information. The younger persons were more active in these respects at secondary and university levels of education. Presumably, the younger educated persons had more to discuss and could get around more to engage in discussions. Activity proved to be a dominant hypothesis.

TABLE 12.1

Belgrade: Knowledge and Decision-Making on Local Problems, by Age (percentages)

Variable	29 and Under	30-59	60+	Significance
Number of local problems				.00*
0-1	12	8	30	
2	24	19	22	
3	33	30	22	
4+	32	43	25	
Number of local solutions				.01
0-1	47	50	65	
2	32	30	18	
3	13	10	8	
4+	8	10	9	
Compares one problem to another	52	61	42	.00*
Attributes for only one problem	15	14	12	n
Problem is important to self	50	40	34	.01
Reasons why problem is important				.00*
0	6	5	25	
1	63	69	59	
2	30	26	15	
3+	1	1	1	

*Significance equals less than .01.

TABLE 12.2

Belgrade: Media Use and Communication on Local Problems, by Age (percentages)

Variable	29 and Under	30-59	60+	Significance
Discussed problem	84	75	71	.01
Attended meeting	25	40	21	.00*
Wanted more information	71	57	41	.00*
Number of sources for local problems				.00*
0-1	22	30	46	
2	22	16	17	
3	20	21	12	
4+	1	1	1	
Mentioned TV	40	41	25	.00*
Mentioned radio	22	26	25	n
Mentioned press	63	56	37	.00*
Mentioned friend	56	39	29	.00*
Mentioned family	14	10	11	n
Mentioned personal experience	85	91	77	.00*
Number of source attributes termed most useful: 1+	70	68	51	.00*

*Significance equals less than .01.

TABLE 12.3

Belgrade: Media Preference on Local Problems, by Age (percentages)

Media Preference	29 and Under	30-59	60+
TV	14	17	11
Radio	2	2	7
Press	38	34	31
Friend	11	7	9
Personal experience	35	40	42

Note: Significance equals .10.

TABLE 12.4

Belgrade: Media Evaluation on Local Problems, by Age (percentages)

Why Useful	29 and Under	30-59	60+
Trust	14	12	6
Availability	39	42	52
Cognitive	30	22	20
Channel	17	24	22

Note: Significance equals n (.2).

TABLE 12.5

Ljubljana: Knowledge and Decision-Making on Local Problems, by Age (percentages)

Variable	29 and Under	30-59	60+	Significance
Number of local problems				.07
0-1	18	19	31	
2	19	19	18	
3	25	25	24	
4+	38	37	28	
Number of local solutions				.03
0-1	54	51	65	
2	27	28	24	
3	9	13	6	
4+	10	8	5	
Compares one problem to another	29	28	32	n
Attributes for only one problem	12	13	13	n
Problem is important to self	52	49	27	.00*
Reasons why problem is important				.02
0	16	17	29	
1	71	72	60	
2	13	11	10	
3+	0	0	1	

*Significance equals less than .01.

TABLE 12.6

Ljubljana: Media Use and Communication on Local Problems, by Age (percentages)

Variable	29 and Under	30-59	60+	Significance
Discussed problem	91	87	84	.21
Attended meeting	28	34	31	n
Wanted more information	77	64	44	.00*
Number of sources for local problems				.01
0-1	34	40	54	
2	14	10	12	
3	20	16	12	
4+	32	34	22	
Mentioned TV	39	35	17	.00*
Mentioned radio	29	29	22	n
Mentioned press	53	48	37	.02
Mentioned friend	41	33	25	.01
Mentioned family	9	9	6	n
Mentioned personal experience	87	85	73	.00*
Number of source attributes termed most useful: 1+	58	54	41	.01

*Significance equals less than .01.

TABLE 12.7

Ljubljana: Media Preference on Local Problems, by Age (percentages)

Media Preference	29 and Under	30-59	60+
TV	14	17	5
Radio	1	1	5
Press	46	38	45
Friend	12	5	7
Personal experience	27	39	38

Note: Significance equals .04.

TABLE 12.8

Ljubljana: Media Evaluation on Local Problems, by Age (percentages)

Why Useful	29 and Under	30-59	60+
Trust	16	13	15
Availability	31	40	36
Cognitive	42	39	40
Channel	11	8	9

Note: Significance equals n.

TABLE 12.9

Seattle: Knowledge and Decision-Making on Local Problems, by Age (percentages)

Variable		29 and Under	30-59	60+	Significance
Number of local problems					n
1		4	5	7	
2		17	14	18	
3+		79	81	76	
Number of local solutions					.00*
0		18	17	27	
1		23	27	35	
2		26	27	23	
3+		33	29	15	
Compares one problem to another	1+	21	18	10	.03
Attributes for only one problem		35	37	39	n
Problem is important to self		58	56	47	.09
Reasons why problem is important					.00*
0		6	3	12	
1		34	37	27	
2		38	36	37	
3+		17	16	14	

*Significance equals less than .01.

TABLE 12.10

Seattle: Media Use and Communication on Local Problems, by Age (percentages)

Variable	29 and Under	30-59	60+	Significance
Discussed problem	90	89	80	.02
Attended meeting	31	40	19	.00*
Wanted more information	70	55	32	.00*
Number of sources for local problems				.00*
0	6	3	12	
1	4	8	6	
2	10	7	18	
3+	79	81	64	
Mentioned TV	63	62	59	n
Mentioned radio	39	40	36	n
Mentioned press	74	77	75	n
Mentioned friend	59	50	40	.00*
Mentioned family	19	20	14	n
Mentioned personal experience	67	66	52	.01
Number of source attributes termed most useful				.00*
0	15	18	28	
1	54	59	56	
2+	31	23	16	

*Significance equals less than .01.

TABLE 12.11

Seattle: Media Preference on Local Problems, by Age (percentages)

Media Preference	29 and Under	30-59	60+
TV	24	20	20
Radio	3	4	6
Press	34	44	50
Friend	14	12	10
Personal experience	25	20	14

Note: Significance equals n (.3).

TABLE 12.12

Seattle: Media Evaluation on Local Problems, by Age (percentages)

Why Useful	29 and Under	30-59	60+
Trust	12	13	8
Availability	0	0	0
Cognitive	39	28	38
Channel	27	31	34

Note: Significance equals n.

CHAPTER

13

AGE ROLE AND WORLD PROBLEMS

As suggested throughout our analysis, world problems demanded more of the individual than did local problems because of their relative complexity and remoteness. Hence we expected the activity potential of youth and the skills of the mid-career groups to assert themselves more strongly. The discrepancies should be greatest in Belgrade because of the lower levels of education of the oldest group there.

BELGRADE

There were distinctive differences in Belgrade in knowledge and decision-making among age groups and, as we expected, these were greater with respect to world problems than local problems. The younger group was most active followed by the mid-career group.

More members of the younger group named more world problems and, like the mid-career group, gave more reasons for the importance of those problems. The younger group offered more sophisticated evaluations as to the nature of problems and, together with the mid-career group, proposed more solutions. In all cases, the oldest group was least knowledgeable and least able to make decisions with respect to world problems.

Greater knowledge and decision-making suggested greater media use and communication as well. More members of the youngest group tended to use more sources of information, television, and interpersonal communication.

The oldest age group made markedly fewer references to media and interpersonal communication and understandably was much less active in discussions at meetings and with families. However, the oldest group reported the greatest personal experience with world problems, these being problems of war and peace. The references, we assumed, were to much earlier experiences.

There were some interesting variations in media evaluation. More members of the two younger age groups were likely to mention television as their most useful source of information. We might have expected the press to be their most useful source since the younger groups were more knowledgeable.

The bases for judging the usefulness of media were interesting because of the preferences for television by the youngest and the mid-career groups.

More members of the oldest group, as we surmised, mentioned availability as a basis for utility. They did not mention channel dimensionalities, for these are usually associated with television and they had less access to television. But, interestingly, although more oriented to television, more members of the two younger groups mentioned informational and channel dimensionalities. Thus these two groups were able to find useful information on television. Apparently they attributed part of that input to the dimensionalities of television.

LJUBLJANA

We did not expect that the findings in Belgrade would hold as strongly for Ljubljana. However, more members of the two younger groups demonstrated an awareness of problems, reasons for the importance of those problems, more sophisticated bases for evaluation, and more solutions. But the discrepancies were not as great as in Belgrade.

However, more members of the youngest age group used more sources of information, including television, press, radio, friendships, family, and interpersonal communication; they also expressed more interest in information. This represented by far the most dramatic differences between age groupings. It suggested that Ljubljana's early-career age group was more deeply involved in world problems than the mid-career group.

Interestingly, the discrepancies in media use were not reflected in media evaluation. There was relative agreement across groups on which media were most useful, with only this difference: Fewer members of the oldest group rated television as most useful, and more of them rated the press as most useful.

There also were few differences in the bases for judging media utility. The oldest group tended more to cite informational reasons, associated with more press use. The press was their primary source of information, and this was therefore understandable. More members of the two younger groups were likely to cite channel characteristics associated with television use.

SEATTLE

Previous data on age roles in American studies have shown the mid-career group to be most involved and concerned about public affairs. The rationale was that, the more individuals were immersed in the work of the society—as expressed in career roles—the more concern they felt with societal problems and needs.

However, in the Belgrade and Ljubljana data there was the suggestion that other processes were at work. Mid-career groups were increasingly concerned with careers and less concerned with the problems of the larger society.

The Seattle data reflected those tendencies. More members of the youngest group named more world problems, tended more to compare problems rather than describe individual problems, and were more able to propose solutions. The youngest group was followed by the mid-career and then the oldest group. Probably Vietnam and world travel of the youngest group were factors in this greater absorption in world affairs.

There were interesting variations in media and communication behavior. For example, the youngest group tended to use more sources of information (slightly more television and slightly less press than the mid-career group). It also tended more to use friends and families as sources of information. Equally with the mid-career group, the youngest group cited personal experience with world problems (these problems tended to be somewhat different, however). The youngest group also referred more to interpersonal communication and was more likely to cite a need for information.

It was also intriguing that the youngest group had a greater tendency to cite the family as a source of information and to describe meetings as a significant source of information and forum for communication.

Nonetheless, more members of the older age groups cited the press as most useful, while fewer cited personal experience. This varied markedly from the Belgrade pattern.

Different criteria for utility were used to judge media with respect to world problems than had been employed for local problems. More members of the oldest group cited trust and availability, which are less discriminating and non-content relevant attributes. The two younger groups cited content and channel characteristics. This was somewhat different than was observed in Ljubljana, where older people tended more to cite content and younger persons to cite channel reasons.

AGE AND EDUCATION

Since education was distributed unequally across the age groupings within each community—and across communities as well—we looked at age roles controlling for education. Again testing the activity hypothesis, we assumed that, given the same level of education, a younger person would be more able to cope with world problems than an elderly person would.

Belgrade

The results were dramatic in two respects with respect to knowledge and decision-making. First, youth was a more significant factor in world problems than in local problems. Second, youth influences were expressed primarily at the lower and secondary levels of education. Where there was a college education, youth was not necessarily served. In effect, college education appeared to overcome the impact of age.

Younger persons at primary and secondary levels of education were more knowledgeable about more problems than older persons and more able to make decisions. But at the university level of education there were almost no differences among age groupings in terms of knowledge and decision-making.

Were these findings expressed in media use and communication? Not necessarily. Television viewing was a common preference of young people without regard to level of education. Nonetheless, the younger groups used more sources of information, including more radio and more press. The greater tendency of older persons at all educational levels to refer to personal experience as a source of knowledge was maintained.

Greater age severely limited interpersonal communication, but higher education helped sustain social contacts. Nonetheless, there was less discussion at meetings by the most highly educated older persons.

Ljubljana

There was a slight modification in the Ljubljana data. The mid-career age role became a somewhat stronger factor with respect to world problems. Nonetheless, the youngest group at primary and secondary levels of education was more knowledgeable and able to make decisions. Most of the differences again disappeared at the university level, where "activity" was extended by education.

Confirmation of the activity hypothesis in media use and communication was striking. Radio, television, and the press all were used more by the younger age groups at all levels of education. The single exception was with respect to the press, where at the university level of education the older groups were as active.

The age role, expressed in prior personal experience, was expressed interestingly in less of a desire for information. An explanation was that the younger groups were concerned with contemporary world problems that demanded more information, whereas the older groups were thinking in terms of earlier events where their previous experience was adequate to define the situation.

Seattle

The picture for Seattle was more mixed than in Ljubljana and Belgrade. Younger persons perceived more world problems at both secondary and university levels, a reversal of some Belgrade and Ljubljana findings.

In Seattle the older persons at the primary level used more media, particularly television, radio, and press. This was a singular finding.

But the younger person at almost all educational levels engaged in more interpersonal discussions, had greater participation in meetings, and wanted more information than the older person did. Here age roles supported our activity hypothesis.

TABLE 13.1

Belgrade: Knowledge and Decision-Making on World Problems, by Age (percentages)

Variable	29 and Under	30-59	60+	Significance
Number of world problems				.00*
0-1	19	25	53	
2	29	31	17	
3	32	26	25	
4+	20	19	6	
Number of world solutions				.00*
0-1	55	55	75	
2	28	28	12	
3	8	7	5	
4+	9	10	8	
Compares one problem to another	61	53	36	.00*
Attributes for only one problem	31	24	18	.02
Problem is important to self	10	18	25	.00*
Reasons why problem is important: 1+	90	86	66	.00*

*Significance equals less than .01.

TABLE 13.2

Belgrade: Media Use and Communication on World Problems, by Age (percentages)

Variable	29 and Under	30-59	60+	Significance
Discussed problem	83	75	69	.01
Attended meeting	38	46	17	.00*
Wanted more information	49	43	41	n
Number of sources for world problems				.00*
0-1	16	22	41	
2	10	10	15	
3	22	23	16	
4+	52	45	28	
Mentioned TV	71	64	40	.00*
Mentioned radio	55	53	35	.00*
Mentioned press	81	76	50	.00*
Mentioned friend	30	27	21	.13
Mentioned family	17	13	6	.01
Mentioned personal experience	14	46	53	.00*
Number of source attributes termed most useful: 1+	76	72	51	.00*

*Significance equals less than.01.

TABLE 13.3

Belgrade: Media Preference on World Problems, by Age (percentages)

Media Evaluation	29 and Under	30-59	60+
TV	42	45	26
Radio	4	4	7
Press	52	42	45
Friend	1	2	2
Personal experience	1	7	20

Note: Significance equals .00 (less than .01).

TABLE 13.4

Belgrade: Media Evaluation on World Problems, by Age (percentages)

Why Useful	29 and Under	30-59	60+
Trust	11	11	3
Availability	12	24	39
Cognitive	37	29	30
Channel	40	36	28

Note: Significance equals .00 (less than .01).

TABLE 13.5

Ljubljana: Knowledge and Decision-Making on World Problems, by Age (percentages)

Variable	29 and Under	30-59	60+	Significance
Number of world problems				.00*
0-1	12	19	34	
2	19	24	20	
3	32	26	22	
4+	37	31	24	
Number of world solutions				.01
0-1	53	46	65	
2	26	29	20	
3	11	12	8	
4+	9	13	6	
Compares one problem to another	47	47	30	.00*
Attributes for only one problem	18	17	14	n
Problem is important to self	20	26	20	.17
Reasons why problem is important: 1+	86	84	62	.00*

*Significance equals less than .01.

TABLE 13.6

Ljubljana: Media Use and Communication on World Problems, by Age (percentages)

Variable	29 and Under	30-59	60+	Significance
Discussed problem	91	87	81	.05
Attended meeting	29	40	30	.02
Wanted more information	59	49	32	.00*
Number of sources for world problems				.00*
0-1	9	19	38	
2	2	6	6	
3	21	16	17	
4+	68	59	38	
Mentioned TV	82	69	41	.00*
Mentioned radio	76	66	45	.00*
Mentioned press	91	81	61	.00*
Mentioned friend	51	32	23	.00*
Mentioned family	23	13	5	.00*
Mentioned personal experience	18	52	50	.00*
Number of source attributes termed most useful: 1+	85	68	46	.00*

*Significance equals less than .01.

TABLE 13.7

Ljubljana: Media Preference on
World Problems, by Age
(percentages)

Media Evaluation	29 and Under	30-59	60+
TV	38	36	19
Radio	9	8	9
Press	48	47	64
Friend	3	2	1
Personal experience	2	7	7

Note: Significance equals .04.

TABLE 13.8

Ljubljana: Media Evaluation on
World Problems, by Age
(percentages)

Why Useful	29 and Under	30-59	60+
Trust	7	9	11
Availability	38	33	35
Cognitive	38	37	45
Channel	17	21	9

Note: Significance equals n (.3).

TABLE 13.9

Seattle: Knowledge and Decision-Making on World Problems, by Age (percentages)

Variable	29 and Under	30-59	60+	Significance
Number of world problems				.00*
1	5	5	12	
2	12	20	24	
3+	83	75	64	
Number of world solutions				.00*
0-1	15	20	30	
2	27	31	30	
3	23	26	28	
4+	35	23	12	
Compares one problem to another	37	28	21	.00*
Attributes for only one problem	39	43	40	n
Problem is important to self	36	36	34	n
Reasons why problem is important				.20
0	18	20	26	
1	29	26	31	
2	39	38	27	
3+	14	16	16	

*Significance equals less than .01.

TABLE 13.10

Seattle: Media Use and Communication on World Problems, by Age (percentages)

Variable	29 and Under	30-59	60+	Significance
Discussed problem	92	86	75	.00*
Attended meeting	46	34	23	.00*
Wanted more information	64	49	29	
Number of sources for world problems				.08
0-1	6	8	9	
2	4	6	8	
3	8	10	16	
4+	82	76	67	
Mentioned TV	72	68	64	.26
Mentioned radio	42	44	50	n
Mentioned press	74	78	82	.19
Mentioned friend	49	42	33	.01
Mentioned family	23	15	16	.08
Mentioned personal experience	50	49	38	.05
Number of source attributes termed most useful				.19
0	13	22	20	
1	62	58	58	
2+	25	20	22	

*Significance equals less than .01.

TABLE 13.11

Seattle: Media Preference on World Problems, by Age (percentages)

Media Evaluation	29 and Under	30-59	60+
TV	30	36	28
Radio	3	1	4
Press	35	49	54
Friend	10	4	4
Personal experience	22	10	10

Note: Significance equals .00 (less than .01).

TABLE 13.12

Seattle: Media Evaluation on World Problems, by Age (percentages)

Why Useful	29 and Under	30-59	60+
Trust	5	8	12
Availability	18	27	34
Cognitive	41	41	33
Channel	36	24	21

Note: Significance equals .05.

CHAPTER

14

INCOME AND LOCAL PROBLEMS

Income as a criterion of communication and decision-making appeared to be a complex variable within cultures as well across cultures.

The lifestyles represented by monthly Yugoslav incomes of 1,000, 2,000, 3,000 and more than 3,000 new dinar per month—our income categories—were difficult to assess.* Comparisons were affected by the number of adults living in the same household, the comparative costs of items, the nature of items deemed indispensables or luxuries in each culture, and a variety of other factors.†

Also, income was distributed differently across the three communities. Belgrade demonstrated the most concentration of income in the lowest category, while Ljubljana and Seattle demonstrated a more homogeneous distribution of income. The discrepancies across cities were quite large. Therefore, for Belgrade we were dealing with a large population in the lowest income category and the smallest population in the highest category, compared to more even distributions for our samples in Ljubljana and Seattle.

---

*These figures are confused further by the fact that (1) the Yugoslavs tend to report their net income rather than their gross income; (2) they do not report other than "formal income." At the time that we did our field work, a dinar was worth about 8 cents.

†For a better comparison of incomes, one must calculate rent at about 10 percent of the American cost (or less), free medical care, and a variety of other benefits.

BELGRADE

Background

Income is not often correlated and reported in studies of media usage in Yugoslavia. Most indications of income and media usage are inferred from data on occupational groupings because income in Yugoslavia is very highly correlated with occupation and education.

Even data for educational groupings in Yugoslavia often are presented in relation to occupational roles. To illustrate, beyond four and eight years of school, educational groupings are defined by those who have secondary vocational training as compared to only worker training. The connection is explicit between educational categories and occupational roles.

As an example of categorization, Danojlić (1965a) found that clerks with post-secondary training—as compared to clerks with only secondary education, craftsmen in private manufacturing jobs, trained workers, and blue-collar workers and assistant clerks—demonstrated the greatest preference for television news. Danojlić (1965b) also found that the post-secondary worker was more interested in the press along most dimensions, but the differences were neither large nor revealing. The pattern for radio also was somewhat mixed, with those of lower occupational skills somewhat more favorably disposed toward radio.

Preference for media followed this pattern in a study by the same author (1965c). Those of higher occupation tended somewhat more to prefer the press and television and somewhat less to prefer radio, but television differences were not great.

Asked how well individuals were politically informed by various mass media sources, Bacević (1965c) found that clerks with post-secondary education, and others with secondary education, tended to rate the media most highly. Occupations were rated by Letica (1966) in terms of how they rated television as a primary source of information. Curiously, more journalists rated television as a primary source, followed by librarians, teachers of various levels of education, professors, craftsmen, and workers.

Finally, Leandrov (1967a) found that, when occupational groupings were asked which of the media they would least give up, there was a mixed picture; evidently television was preferred for entertainment, while the press was most useful for information—the latter among the higher occupational groupings.

In these studies, news was defined as a general classification rather than with reference to a specific problem—local or world—at a particular time. And different investigators used different classification schemes for occupational groupings. Each cited occupational groupings rather than income levels.

Findings

In our own data there was a strong association of knowledge and decision-making with income in Belgrade. Those of higher income were more likely to name more problems (discrepancies were greatest at the lowest income level), to give more reasons why problems were important, to propose more solutions (most apparent among those of the highest income), and to compare one problem with another (those of lowest income were least able to engage in comparisons).

There also were relationships with media use and communication. As would be expected, those of higher income used more sources of information, and specifically used television and the press more. Friendships were markedly less mentioned by those of the lowest income; personal experience also was less cited. However, there were no differences by income groupings in use of radio, and there were only slight differences in use of family members as sources of information. Interestingly, those of lowest income referred least to family contacts.

Those of higher income had a richer fund of social contacts. They discussed problems more with others and also discussed problems more at meetings. Therefore, it was not unexpected that those of the lowest income were least likely to think that more information would be useful to them. They used it less.

Those of lower income tended slightly more to name television as most useful. Considering the relative lack of accessibility to television, this was significant. By contrast, many more of those of higher income named the press as most useful. As to why sources of information were most useful, those of higher income tended more to cite the media as useful because of their content and less because of their availability. The influence of education probably was felt here.

LJUBLJANA

Background

A number of early studies on the ownership and use of media reflect broader access to and availability of radio and television in Ljubljana. The Kroflič, Obranović, et al 1967 study of television in Slovenia found income to be highly correlated with ownership of television sets. Only 5 percent of those who earned less than 1,000 dinars per month owned television sets, compared to 38 percent of those earning up to 4,000 dinars and 67 percent up to 7,000 dinars. About two-thirds of those in white-collar occupations and students owned television sets, compared with about 40 percent of skilled laborers and 30 percent of unskilled laborers and retired persons.

The Kroflič, Meseč, et al 1967 radio study showed that 74 percent of the white-collar workers owned both radio and television, compared with slightly more than 50 percent of skilled and unskilled laborers.

Those of middle income tended to spend more time watching television. The least viewing was done by those of the lowest income, followed by those of the highest income.

Interestingly, there was a strong correlation with occupation in the viewing of foreign television. Highly skilled laborers and white-collar workers viewed more Italian and Austrian television than did housewives, retired persons, or peasants. White-collar workers were more attuned to Italian television and highly skilled laborers were more attuned to Austrian television.

With respect to the press, a large proportion of those in higher managerial functions read Delo and Dnevnik than those of lower managerial functions. This was most dramatically true for Delo; it was not true for Vecer.

Findings

As in Belgrade, we expected relationships between income, knowledge and decision-making, and media use and communication. But, because of the greater homogeneity in income among our Ljubljana groupings, we did not expect great discrepancies.

Those of higher income were more aware of problems and gave more reasons for the importance of local problems, although not to the extent noted in Belgrade; this was consistent with our expectations. Higher income groups also proposed more solutions and engaged in more comparisons of one problem to another, but again, markedly less than in Belgrade.

In Ljubljana more of the higher income groups used a greater number of sources of information, although fewer than in Belgrade. The higher income groups used television more, cited the press more often, and gave more reasons for the usefulness of media, but with less frequency than in Belgrade.

Use of friends, family, and personal experience as sources of information did not differ greatly by income levels. Thus, income homogeneity limited the variations in media use.

However, more of those of higher income cited the press as most useful and personal experience as less useful. The discrepancies were much greater in Ljubljana than in Belgrade. Thus, income was more strongly associated with sophistication in media use. There also were significant differences in among income groups in judging why media were more useful. Those of higher income tended much more to use content criteria, while those of lower incomes judged media to be most useful because of their availability.

We thus observed the interesting finding that homogeneity of income was related to homogeneity in knowledge and decision-making in Ljubljana, but there were countertendencies present in media use and evaluation. Apparently the nature of decisions and the inputs of media into those decisions were affected by levels of income. More income predicted not only more access to the media but also different uses—or functions—for the media.

SEATTLE

Background

Turning to Seattle, we conjectured that income should be less of a factor in defining orientations to local problems—not only because of the more equal distribution of education across income levels but also because of the nature of the local problems in Seattle, particularly unemployment.

We examined several earlier studies summarizing media use and evaluation by income levels that were relevant to our own data. Media access does not vary in the United States for television, radio, or the press by economic levels to any significant extent other than for numbers of radio or color television sets in a single household. Newspaper use is slightly correlated with income levels.

Greenberg and Dervin (1967), for example, compared low income and general population respondents and found that low income persons had as many black-and-white but fewer color television sets; they also liked television more. Interestingly, they read the newspaper less than the general population, but not dramatically so. They preferred television much more for nonlocal news and preferred newspapers much less. They preferred television somewhat more for local news and newspapers significantly less. They also depended more on talking to people for local news.

A very mixed pattern of television news viewing was associated with income in the national newspaper reading study conducted in 1971. The middle income group watched the least television news, while the lower and higher income groupings watched the most. There was no explanation for this seeming inconsistency in pattern.

In the ANPA study carried out in 1971, the highest income group tended to be more critical of their daily newspaper. Westley and Severin (1964b) found that nonreaders of newspapers tended to be laborers and farmers, followed by clerical/sales personnel and managers and proprietors, and as a third group, professionals.

Findings

With respect to knowledge and decision-making, the differences across income levels for Seattle were less marked. More of those of higher income were only somewhat more likely to name more local problems. They failed to give more reasons for the importance of problems, and they consistently failed to give more solutions. However, those of higher income did tend more to compare one problem to another as a means of evaluating it. But, as an isolated instance of decision-making, this was inconclusive.

One explanation of the Seattle data was the character of the most important local problem—unemployment. This affected all income levels, from the Boeing engineer to the blue-collar worker.

Similar cognitive behavior suggested fewer discrepancies in media use and communication. However, more of those of higher income did use more sources of information. More used the press (but the discrepancy held only between the lowest and highest income groups) and television, but this was discrepant only with respect to the lowest income group. There were no differences in use of friends, family, and personal experience as sources of information.

Income had powerful effects with respect to social communication, however. Those of higher income engaged in more interpersonal discussion and also in discussion at meetings. Evidently, income permitted a higher degree of social movement.

There was a slight tendency also for higher income respondents to cite the press as most useful. Lower-income persons were more likely to cite personal experience as their most useful source. This would reflect less economic access to media.

Extended to reasons why media were more or less useful, there was a slight tendency for persons of higher income to cite availability criteria, but this was not a significant difference. However, it is consistent with a hypothesis based on economic access.

INCOME AND EDUCATION

Because education was a significant factor, we asked whether any differences would persist that might be attributed to income levels alone. Did people actually behave in some ways because of their income, or could these differences be attributed largely to education?

Belgrade

There was, at primary levels of education, a tendency for those of higher income in Belgrade to have more solutions for problems, but behavior did not otherwise differ. Income had few facilitating effects at the lowest level of education.

At the secondary level of education, however, those of higher income mentioned more problems, in most cases described problems more fully, and proposed more solutions. Thus income had some facilitating effects at the secondary level of education.

At the university level, interestingly, there were no differences in behavior by income roles. In fact, lower income people of high education cited more local problems than middle and higher income people of high education. Thus low income actually modified the behavior of those of high education.

Media use and communication did not follow this pattern entirely. At the primary level of education, the higher income people reported more use of television and newspapers. Thus, income permitted media access and, consequently, use. This was more strongly evident at the secondary level of education, but it again did not hold at the university level.

More of the higher income persons engaged in discussion, attended meetings, and consulted friends at both the primary and secondary levels. Thus income permitted more social movement. Again, there was no evidence of an income effect for persons of high education. Apparently, high education produced social movement without high income.

Ljubljana

In Ljubljana those of higher income cited more local problems at the primary level of education, but the income effect was not quite as strong as in Belgrade. This picture also continued at the secondary level of education. Again, as in Belgrade, at the university level there were no differences attributable to income roles.

The only media distinction at the primary level of education was in greater use of television by those of higher income. In this important media respect, income was facilitative. Higher income persons at the primary and secondary levels of education wanted more information. Otherwise, there was no evidence of an income effect.

Seattle

We began to surmise that there would be even fewer income effects in Seattle. This would be due to the more even distribution of income across education. In fact, the only discernible difference was that higher income persons engaged in significantly more discussion, due probably to the social mobility that higher income affords.

TABLE 14.1

Belgrade: Knowledge and Decision-Making on Local Problems, by Income (percentages)

Variable	Income Level				Significance
	1,000 ND	2,000 ND	3,000 ND	3,000+ND	
Number of local problems					.03
1	12	6	5	5	
2	23	23	22	17	
3+	65	71	73	78	
Number of local solutions					.00*
1	55	51	47	35	
2	26	31	31	32	
3+	19	18	22	33	
Compares one problem to another	46	57	60	63	.01
Attribute for only one problem	13	13	15	14	n
Problem is important to self	41	37	39	49	.20
Reasons why problem is important					.00*
0	17	8	4	4	
1	61	67	72	60	
2	21	24	23	35	
3+	1	1	1	1	

*Significance equals less than .01.

TABLE 14.2

Belgrade: Media Use and Communication on Local Problems, by Income (percentages)

Variable	Income Level 1,000 ND	2,000 ND	3,000 ND	3,000+ND	Significance
Discussed problem	66	76	85	79	.00*
Attended meeting	20	36	35	45	.00*
Wanted more information	49	61	59	59	.04
Number of sources for local problems					.01
1	33	26	19	18	
2	20	15	21	23	
3+	47	59	60	59	
Mentioned TV	30	38	44	43	.02
Mentioned radio	27	24	26	26	n
Mentioned press	40	53	64	61	.00*
Mentioned friend	27	44	44	47	.00*
Mentioned family	6	11	13	17	.02
Mentioned personal experience	83	87	90	92	.04
Number of source attributes termed most useful					.00*
0	48	33	27	26	
1+	52	67	73	74	

*Significance equals less than .01.

TABLE 14.3

Belgrade: Media Preference on Local Problems, by Income (percentages)

Media Evaluation	Income Level			
	1,000 ND	2,000 ND	3,000 ND	3,000 ND+
TV	18	16	15	12
Radio	3	3	3	0
Press	26	32	39	43
Friend	5	9	8	7
Personal experience	48	40	35	38

Note: Significance equals n.

TABLE 14.4

Belgrade: Media Evaluation on Local Problems, by Income (percentages)

Why Useful	Income Level			
	1,000 ND	2,000 ND	3,000 ND	3,000 ND+
Trust	12	11	11	13
Availability	52	47	31	40
Cognitive	17	20	35	23
Channel	19	22	23	24

Note: Significance equals .03.

TABLE 14.5

Ljubljana: Knowledge and Decision-Making on Local Problems, by Income (percentages)

Variable	Income Level				Significance
	1,000 ND	2,000 ND	3,000 ND	3,000+ND	
Number of local problems					.00*
1	26	14	10	7	
2	31	21	22	15	
3+	43	65	68	78	
Number of local solutions					.02
1	58	52	41	41	
2	28	27	39	32	
3+	14	21	20	27	
Compares one problem to another	15	33	28	33	.01
Attribute for only one problem	16	12	13	12	n
Problem is important to self	42	41	48	48	n
Reasons why problem is important					.02
0	30	19	19	15	
1	63	72	67	72	
2	7	8	14	13	
3+	0	1	0	0	

*Significance equals less than .01.

TABLE 14.6

Ljubljana: Media Use and Communication on Local Problems, by Income (percentages)

Variable	Income Level				Significance
	1,000 ND	2,000 ND	3,000 ND	3,000+ND	
Discussed problem	82	85	88	90	.20
Attended meeting	29	29	28	40	.04
Wanted more information	55	60	67	66	.20
Number of sources for local problems					.10
1	47	36	34	29	
2	14	12	12	13	
3+	39	52	54	58	
Mentioned TV	14	31	38	35	.00*
Mentioned radio	20	28	26	32	.20
Mentioned press	30	43	48	56	.00*
Mentioned friend	27	34	31	35	n
Mentioned family	4	8	8	10	n
Mentioned personal experience	73	83	85	86	.03
Number of source attributes termed most useful					.00*
0	61	53	47	39	
1	39	47	53	61	
2+	0	0	0	0	

*Significance equals less than .01.

TABLE 14.7

Ljubljana: Media Preference on Local Problems, by Income (percentages)

Media Evaluation	Income Level 1,000 ND	2,000 ND	3,000 ND	3,000 ND+
TV	10	15	18	13
Radio	7	4	0	0
Press	23	35	38	55
Friend	7	5	6	6
Personal experience	53	41	38	26

Note: Significance equals .01.

TABLE 14.8

Ljubljana: Media Evaluation on Local Problems, by Income (percentages)

Why Useful	Income Level 1,000 ND	2,000 ND	3,000 ND	3,000 ND+
Trust	4	19	17	10
Availability	63	40	35	29
Cognitive	20	35	34	54
Channel	13	6	14	7

Note: Significance equals .00 (less than .01).

TABLE 14.9

Seattle: Knowledge and Decision-Making on Local Problems, by Income (percentages)

Variable	Income Level				Significance
	$5,000	$10,000	$15,000	$15,000+	
Number of local problems					.06
1	6	4	2	6	
2	21	14	16	8	
3+	73	83	82	86	
Number of local solutions					.22
1	42	26	35	35	
2	32	36	32	31	
3+	26	38	33	34	
Compares one problem to another	10	20	20	27	.01
Attribute for only one problem	39	49	52	56	.03
Problem is important to self	50	59	59	46	.10
Reasons why problem is important					.10
0	21	10	11	15	
1	35	39	39	31	
2	35	38	42	45	
3+	9	13	8	9	

TABLE 14.10

Seattle: Media Use and Communication on Local Problems, by Income (percentages)

Variable	Income Level				Significance
	$5,000	$10,000	$15,000	$15,000+	
Discussed problem	81	88	93	97	.00*
Attended meeting	25	26	41	57	.00*
Wanted more information	55	52	59	53	n
Number of sources for local problems					.06
1	5	8	6	3	
2	16	5	9	9	
3+	79	87	85	88	
Mentioned TV	55	69	68	65	.02
Mentioned radio	38	44	39	38	n
Mentioned press	67	80	81	87	.00*
Mentioned friend	49	54	50	57	n
Mentioned family	18	19	20	19	n
Mentioned personal experience	63	65	59	68	n
Number of source attributes termed most useful					.00*
0	30	17	14	10	
1+	70	83	86	90	

*Significance equals less than .01.

TABLE 14.11

Seattle: Media Preference on Local Problems, by Income (percentages)

Media Evaluation	Income Level			
	$5,000	$10,000	$15,000	$15,000+
TV	19	22	26	17
Radio	4	5	5	4
Press	37	43	45	47
Friend	16	10	12	14
Personal experience	24	20	12	18

Note: Significance equals n.

TABLE 14.12

Seattle: Media Evaluation on Local Problems, by Income (percentages)

Why Useful	Income Level			
	$5,000	$10,000	$15,000	$15,000+
Trust	12	11	19	6
Availability	20	22	29	30
Cognitive	31	41	33	30
Channel	37	26	19	34

Note: Significance equals .20.

CHAPTER

15

INCOME AND WORLD PROBLEMS

BELGRADE

We expected income to have greater relevance to world problems, since income should permit more access to media, to travel, and to personal experience.

More of those of the highest income did indeed name more world problems. Generally, income groupings differed more in their behavior with respect to world problems than for local problems.

More of those of higher income also demonstrated greater media use and communication, including the press, television, and radio.

Finally, those of higher income engaged in appreciably more interpersonal discussion and discussion at meetings, and also expressed more of an interest in information. This supports a mobility hypothesis for income.

There also was a greater correspondence between higher income and citing the press as most useful. More of those of higher income also tended to cite content reasons—a more discriminating evaluation—and fewer tended to cite availability as a reason for media utility—a less discriminating one.

LJUBLJANA

We were curious about the effects that generally higher levels of income and more equal distribution of income should have in Ljubljana.

Those of higher income named significantly more world problems than did those of lower income, and also named significantly more reasons why problems were important. Contrary to Belgrade, they accorded more importance to world problems than to local problems. They provided more solutions and tended much more to compare one world problem to another as a means of coming to a solution. Thus the income effect was more pronounced in Ljubljana than in Belgrade.

The greater concern about world problems carried with it greater media use and communication. Those of higher income named appreciably more sources of information. Among media, they used television and radio more, cited the press even more dramatically, and named friendship sources more often, a finding quite discrepant from that observed for local problems. The mobility function of income appeared to be quite significant in Ljubljana.

Interestingly, differences in media evaluation appeared only with respect to television. Apparently the impact of income, as compared to education, had little effect on the nature of discrimination among media.

SEATTLE

The more even distribution of education across groups in Seattle created the probability that the income variable would be less predictive. There were indeed fewer relationships between level of income and decision-making. Those of higher income did not name more world problems. They gave slightly more reasons why world problems were important and proposed more solutions, but this characterized primarily the middle income groups.

Overall, the picture was one of somewhat more activity by those of middle income, possibly correlated with higher levels of education. It was notable that the pattern differed substantially from that observed for local problems, where income was a more linearly related function.

We might assume that media use and communication would roughly parallel knowledge and decision-making. But more of those of higher income did not use appreciably more sources of information. That is a provocative finding not present so clearly in the other cities.

Even in the realm of social communication in Seattle, there were no substantial differences attributed to income levels.

Mixed influences were seen again in the lack of relationship between income and media evaluation. There was only correspondence between citing of newspapers and higher income. It was quite possible that Vietnam might have had a homogenizing effect on use and evaluation of media by income levels.

INCOME AND EDUCATION

We sought to determine if income could demonstrate any independent effects for world problems. We therefore looked at income levels at each educational level.

Belgrade

At the primary level of education in Belgrade, the higher income persons proposed more problems, described problems more fully, and suggested more solutions. The effect was even more pronounced at the secondary level of education. However, the effects were least pronounced, and least stable, at the university level. We therefore reasoned that education diminished the income effect with respect to behavior.

With more income there was more media use and communication at both the primary and secondary levels of education, particularly with respect to television and the press. The lowest income people were less able to evaluate the utility of media; also, more of those of higher income attended meetings where world problems were discussed. Thus income produced access to social groups.

At the secondary level, those of moderate income were the most active in attending meetings and wanting information, but they were not not more attendant to media. And at the university level, again, income did not assert itself.

The middle-income person at the secondary level of education appeared to be most conscious of media and communication. Highly integrated into their social groupings, they were more oriented to social problems of all kinds.

Ljubljana

In Ljubljana, there was not a large uneducated group, as in Belgrade, that would be unable to utilize income in socially integrated ways, but there was a tendency at the primary and secondary levels of education for higher income persons to name more problems and describe problems more fully. The higher income persons at the secondary level also suggested more solutions. At the university level of education, there was no income role. This was consistent with the Belgrade pattern.

At the primary and secondary levels of education, higher income persons used more television, radio, and newspapers. But this finding again did not demonstrate itself at the university level.

The family was more of a source of information for higher income persons at primary and secondary levels of education, but there was no consistent pattern of discussion with others, attending meetings, or wanting information.

Seattle

There was no consistent evidence of an income role in Seattle, although there were scattered effects. The same conditions held true across all variables.

CONCLUSION

Overall, income role was a more significant force in our two Yugoslav cities than in Seattle. Income, we concluded, was a provocative longitudinal variable. Effects of increased income should be studied over time as a development concept.

TABLE 15.1

Belgrade: Knowledge and Decision-Making on World Problems, by Income (percentages)

Variable	Income Level				Significance
	1,000 ND	2,000 ND	3,000 ND	3,000+ND	
Number of world problems					.00*
1	21	22	12	14	
2	42	31	32	24	
3+	37	47	56	62	
Number of world solutions					
1	56	54	49	44	.05
2	21	31	31	33	
3+	23	15	20	23	
Compares one problem to another	35	55	56	60	.00*
Attribute for only one problem	22	21	32	27	.02
Problem is important to self	21	18	14	19	.20
Reasons why problem is important					.00*
0	30	17	9	7	
1	70	83	91	93	

*Significance equals less than .01.

TABLE 15.2

Belgrade: Media Use and Communication on World Problems, by Income (percentages)

Variable	Income Level 1,000 ND	2,000 ND	3,000 ND	3,000+ND	Significance
Discussed problem	60	73	84	88	.00*
Attended meeting	19	39	48	54	.00*
Wanted more information	36	48	41	50	.04
Number of sources for world problems					.01
1	18	12	7	7	
2	13	12	10	17	
3+	69	76	83	76	
Mentioned TV	44	63	72	68	.00*
Mentioned radio	40	51	59	56	.00*
Mentioned press	52	72	86	88	.00*
Mentioned friend	23	29	27	27	n
Mentioned family	11	11	15	16	n
Mentioned personal experience	36	39	43	43	n
Number of source attributes termed most useful					.00*
0	45	24	14	10	
1+	55	76	86	90	

*Significance equals less than .01.

TABLE 15.3

Belgrade: Media Preference on World Problems, by Income (percentages)

Media Evaluation	Income Level			
	1,000 ND	2,000 ND	3,000 ND	3,000 ND+
TV	43	46	37	33
Radio	8	6	3	2
Press	31	40	53	59
Friend	4	1	1	3
Personal experience	14	7	6	3

Note: Significance equals .00 (less than .01).

TABLE 15.4

Belgrade: Media Evaluation on World Problems, by Income (percentages)

Why Useful	Income Level			
	1,000 ND	2,000 ND	3,000 ND	3,000 ND+
Trust	6	11	10	10
Availability	25	26	21	16
Cognitive	29	27	34	41
Channel	40	36	35	33

Note: Significance equals n.

TABLE 15.5

Ljubljana: Knowledge and Decision-Making on World Problems, by Income (percentages)

Variable	Income Level				Significance
	1,000 ND	2,000 ND	3,000 ND	3,000+ND	
Number of world problems					.00*
1	27	12	10	10	
2	27	25	31	17	
3+	46	63	59	73	
Number of world solutions					.08
1	50	45	41	38	
2	30	36	28	33	
3+	20	19	31	29	
Compares one problem to another	23	38	48	53	.00*
Attribute for only one problem	12	20	17	15	n
Problem is important to self	23	24	23	25	n
Reasons why problem is important					.00*
0	42	23	13	14	
1	58	77	87	86	

*Significance equals less than .01.

TABLE 15.6

Ljubljana: Media Use and Communication on World Problems, by Income (percentages)

Variable	Income Level				Significance
	1,000 ND	2,000 ND	3,000 ND	3,000+ND	
Discussed problem	82	85	83	93	.01
Attended meeting	22	33	38	41	.03
Wanted more information	38	44	50	54	.08
Number of sources for world problems					.01
1	25	13	9	8	
2	8	7	6	5	
3+	67	80	85	87	
Mentioned TV	31	63	76	75	.00*
Mentioned radio	42	65	68	69	.00*
Mentioned press	48	73	87	90	.00*
Mentioned friend	22	33	37	36	.07
Mentioned family	4	10	16	18	.00*
Mentioned personal experience	46	44	44	47	n
Number of source attributes termed most useful					.00*
0	57	29	22	17	
1	43	71	78	83	

*Significance equals less than .01.

TABLE 15.7

Ljubljana: Media Preference on World Problems, by Income (percentages)

Media Evaluation	Income Level 1,000 ND	2,000 ND	3,000 ND	3,000 ND+
TV	16	35	42	29
Radio	19	12	6	5
Press	56	45	44	59
Friend	0	2	1	3
Personal experience	9	6	7	4

Note: Significance equals .00 (less than .01).

TABLE 15.8

Ljubljana: Media Evaluation on World Problems, by Income (percentages)

Why Useful	Income Level 1,000 ND	2,000 ND	3,000 ND	3,000 ND+
Trust	10	7	11	9
Availability	33	42	31	31
Cognitive	40	37	35	42
Channel	17	14	23	18

Note: Significance equals n.

TABLE 15.9

Seattle: Knowledge and Decision-Making on World Problems, by Income (percentages)

Variable	Income Level $5,000	$10,000	$15,000	$15,000+	Significance
Number of world problems					.03
1	11	3	4	5	
2	18	16	15	24	
3+	71	81	81	71	
Number of world solutions					.01
1	46	38	35	25	
2	30	24	31	48	
3+	24	38	34	27	
Compares one problem to another	23	30	32	44	.01
Attribute for only one problem	47	57	58	41	.03
Problem is important to self	33	37	33	37	n
Reasons why problem is important					.10
0	27	18	21	16	
1	73	82	79	84	

TABLE 15.10

Seattle: Media Use and Communication on World Problems, by Income (percentages)

Variable	Income Level				Significance
	$5,000	$10,000	$15,000	$15,000+	
Discussed problem	83	86	88	90	n
Attended meeting	34	33	42	44	.20
Wanted more information	52	48	54	42	n
Number of sources for world problems					n
1	7	4	5	5	
2	14	10	8	10	
3+	79	86	87	85	
Mentioned TV	64	71	70	70	n
Mentioned radio	42	47	50	46	n
Mentioned press	69	83	84	84	.00*
Mentioned friend	43	47	41	32	.20
Mentioned family	17	16	17	21	n
Mentioned personal experience	42	45	45	65	.02
Number of source attributes termed most useful					n
0	21	18	16	19	
1	79	82	84	81	

*Significance equals less than .01.

TABLE 15.11

Seattle: Media Preference on World Problems, by Income (percentages)

Media Evaluation	Income Level $5,000	$10,000	$15,000	$15,000+
TV	28	37	32	26
Radio	3	3	2	0
Press	41	41	55	61
Friend	11	6	1	0
Personal experience	17	13	10	13

Note: Significance equals .02.

TABLE 15.12

Seattle: Media Evaluation on World Problems, by Income (percentages)

Why Useful	Income Level $5,000	$10,000	$15,000	$15,000+
Trust	11	6	9	4
Availability	26	21	27	30
Cognitive	36	42	31	39
Channel	26	31	34	26

Note: Significance equals n.

PART IV

COGNITIVE VARIABLES

CHAPTER

16

PROBLEMS, DECISION-MAKING, AND COMMUNICATION

We were interested in the extent to which media usage and other communication were associated with the number of problems, that is, the number of focal objects the individual maintained in his psychological field.

Our interest in getting a tentative answer to this question stemmed from a desire to compare the findings generated by our methodological approach to findings produced by other more conventional approaches.

Conventional studies, such as those conducted by the American Newspaper Publishers Association and Opinion Research Corporation, reported earlier, asked respondents about their attention to "local news" and "world news." Thus they asked about exposure to a "category" of news rather than to a particular item, or problem, within a category. While it would seem that attention to a category of news would be greater than attention to a single item, or problem, there was a predictive equation that might emerge. Stated as a question, it would be:

Did media use and other communication increase markedly when a person was concerned with two or more problems—rather than only one problem? If there were few differences in media use and other communication as the individual moved from consideration of a single-object to multi-objects, media behavior reported for a single problem could be an indication of the respondent's use of the media for a number of problems.

We had asked respondents about two problems: a local problem and a world problem. Could media behavior with respect to these two focal objects be considered a reliable index of total media behavior?

LOCAL PROBLEMS

Belgrade

We observed in Belgrade that there was an increased use of media with an increase from two to three focal objects. There was use of a greater number of sources, particularly television, the press, and interpersonal communication. Thus, to estimate total media use for local problems in Belgrade would require data with regard to three focal objects rather than one or two focal objects.

Ljubljana

In Ljubljana, in contrast to Belgrade, there was no greater use of media with an increase from two to three focal objects. The greatest increment occurred from one to two local problems. This was true for number of sources, television, radio, press, friends, and family. Observation of two focal objects thus provided an adequate measurement of media use in relation to any number of focal objects in Ljubljana.

Seattle

In Seattle, the greatest increment of media use and communication occurred from one to two focal objects. That is, there was much more use of television, radio, press, and number of sources for those who cited two problems rather than one problem, but there was no appreciable increase in media use for those who cited three or more problems. This permitted an estimate of the individual's total media use on the basis of his orientation to two local problems.

WORLD PROBLEMS

Since world problems were more removed, we assumed the individual was more dependent upon media. Hence, world problems represented a more exacting test of our approach.

Belgrade

But, once again, in Belgrade the most substantial differences in media use occurred where the individual increased his awareness from one to two world problems. The person who cited two problems was much more likely to use television, radio, press, and family as sources of information. Use of social communication also increased as the number of world problems increased. But a "two-object prediction" could be made for friends, interpersonal communication, discussion at meetings, and wanting more information.

Ljubljana

In Ljubljana, there was a steady, although not large, increment of media behavior in increased attention given to three world problems. Number of sources, television, radio, press, interpersonal discussion, and attending meetings all were referred to significantly more by those who were aware of three or more problems.

Seattle

In Seattle, the use of the press, television, family, personal experience, and interpersonal communication all increased significantly with increases to three rather than two focal objects. But the only differences with respect to radio were between one and two focal objects. Thus in Seattle one could not predict media behavior in relation to one or two focal objects. Media use increased as the number of focal objects increased.

CONCLUSIONS

Overall, media behavior with respect to one, two, and at the most three local and world problems appeared to reflect media behavior with respect to any number of problems. Thus, accurate projections of media use may be gained from highly situational, object-centered studies. Attitudinal, non-object-centered investigations may not be the best means of establishing the extent and kind of individual media use.

TABLE 16.1

Belgrade: Number of Local Problems as Related to Media Use and Communication (percentages)

Variable	Number of Local Problems			Significance
	1	2	3+	
Discussed problem	62	69	80	.00*
Attended meeting	22	28	37	.01
Wanted more information	39	46	63	.00*
Number of sources for local problems				.00*
0	0	2	4	
1	45	33	19	
2	23	24	16	
3+	32	41	61	
Mentioned TV	17	29	46	.00*
Mentioned radio	12	21	30	.00*
Mentioned press	32	45	63	.00*
Mentioned friend	25	36	47	.00*
Mentioned family	10	10	13	n
Mentioned personal experience	97	95	92	.19

*Significance equals less than .01.

TABLE 16.2

Ljubljana: Number of Local Problems as Related to Media Use and Communication (percentages)

Variable	Number of Local Problems			Significance
	1	2	3+	
Discussed problem	82	84	89	.07
Attended meeting	21	25	36	.00*
Wanted more information	64	63	63	n
Number of sources for local problems				.01
0	2	1	1	
1	52	33	31	
2	12	15	12	
3+	33	50	56	
Mentioned TV	23	32	39	.01
Mentioned radio	20	32	32	.09
Mentioned press	35	48	56	.00*
Mentioned friend	24	39	38	.04
Mentioned family	4	10	10	.15
Mentioned personal experience	88	91	93	n

*Significance equals less than .01.

TABLE 16.3

Seattle: Number of Local Problems as Related to Media Use and Communication (percentages)

Variable	Number of Local Problems 1	2	3+	Significance
Discussed problem	87	76	90	.00*
Attended meeting	13	11	38	.00*
Wanted more information	47	41	58	.01
Number of sources for local problems				.00*
0	0	0	2	
1	20	6	6	
2	40	21	8	
3+	40	72	85	
Mentioned TV	40	62	67	.01
Mentioned radio	27	38	42	.21
Mentioned press	50	69	83	.00*
Mentioned friend	47	53	54	n
Mentioned family	10	9	22	.00*
Mentioned personal experience	60	63	67	n

*Significance equals less than .01.

TABLE 16.4

Belgrade: Number of World Problems as Related to Media Use and Communication (percentages)

Variable	Number of World Problems			Significance
	1	2	3+	
Discussed problem	63	73	82	.00*
Attended meeting	29	36	47	.00*
Wanted more information	30	41	51	.00*
Number of sources for world problems				.00*
0	3	2	3	
1	17	13	8	
2	16	15	9	
3+	65	70	80	
Mentioned TV	61	69	74	.01
Mentioned radio	47	60	60	.01
Mentioned press	75	82	86	.01
Mentioned friend	19	28	36	.00*
Mentioned family	9	14	17	.06
Mentioned personal experience	51	43	45	n

*Significance equals less than .01.

TABLE 16.5

Ljubljana: Number of World Problems as Related to Media Use and Communication (percentages)

Variable	Number of World Problems 1	2	3+	Significance
Discussed problem	71	83	92	.00*
Attended meeting	21	32	40	.00*
Wanted more information	40	47	50	.23
Number of sources for world problems				.00*
0	4	2	2	
1	29	12	8	
2	12	7	4	
3+	56	79	87	
Mentioned TV	56	69	77	.00*
Mentioned radio	51	66	76	.00*
Mentioned press	72	84	90	.00*
Mentioned friend	31	33	40	.14
Mentioned family	13	13	15	n
Mentioned personal experience	47	50	50	n

*Significance equals less than .01.

TABLE 16.6

Seattle: Number of World Problems as Related to Media Use and Communication (percentages)

Variable	Number of World Problems			Significance
	1	2	3+	
Discussed problem	72	83	87	.03
Attended meeting	23	24	40	.00*
Wanted more information	41	42	53	.06
Number of sources for world problems				.00*
0	3	4	4	
1	15	10	4	
2	28	16	9	
3+	55	71	84	
Mentioned TV	50	72	73	.01
Mentioned radio	38	40	50	.07
Mentioned press	68	75	84	.01
Mentioned friend	48	33	46	.04
Mentioned family	5	17	20	.07
Mentioned personal experience	45	45	51	n

*Significance equals less than .01.

CHAPTER

17

KNOWLEDGE AND COMMUNICATION

"Attributes" was the term we used to describe the means by which our respondents described local and world problems. Attributes might be statements or bits of information that defined, explained, or in other ways told about the nature of the problems. Thus the number and quality of attributes represented the sum of an individual's relevant knowledge about a problem or focal object at that time. (More carefully stated, it would be the sum of the knowledge that we were able to elicit at that time.)

We utilized quantitative and qualitative measures of relevant knowledge or attributes:

- Quantitatively, an individual who made three or more statements about the importance of a problem (provided three or more attributes) was more knowledgeable than an individual who made only one or two statements about the problem.
- Qualitatively, an individual who compared two or more objects on a single dimension (example: one problem is more costly than another problem) was different from an individual who used attributes to distinguish objects (example: pollution creates health disorders, while traffic makes one late for work).

Our analysis looked only at the quantitative dimensions of knowledge; that is, it asked if having greater knowledge permitted individuals to engage in decision-making and/or resulted in different use and evaluation of mass media and communication.

LOCAL PROBLEMS

Belgrade

Surprisingly, in Belgrade there were no differences in ability to provide solutions for local problems—that is, in decision-making—among those with more quantitative knowledge about problems.

We speculated that it might require fewer attributes to make decisions about local problems because of the opportunities for validation of one's judgments by personal observation—one did not need as much media-derived knowledge. More important, one could, by personal observation, test one attribute at a time, one reason for doing something at a time. One reason could be enough, if validated by personal observation.

Consistent with these expectations, there was only a slight tendency for people with different numbers of attributes to have different patterns of media use and communication. The only exception was that the press was used somewhat more by those who were most informed and those with more knowledge were more likely to discuss problems. They also tended more to want information.

Ljubljana

In contrast to Belgrade, having greater knowledge in Ljubljana was related positively to decision-making; that is, those with the most knowledge were able to offer more solutions for local problems. The nature of local problems in Ljubljana might have promised more utility for knowledge, and generally higher levels of education also permitted more decision-making as a function of knowledge.

Knowledge also was related to media use and communication, suggesting that media were relevant sources of information. This was reflected in the additional finding that those with the most knowledge also were most able to evaluate the utility of media. The sources of information that were most highly correlated with knowledge were television, the press, and friends.

There were no differences among those with more or less knowledge with respect to interpersonal communication, meetings, or wanting more information. The lack of differences was due, in part, to the very high levels of interpersonal communication among all respondents in Ljubljana.

Seattle

We looked for the tendencies noted in Ljubljana to hold more strongly in Seattle, and those who were the most knowledgeable did tend most to have solutions for local problems. Those in Seattle who were the most knowledgeable also engaged in the greatest media use and communication and were most able to evaluate the utility of those sources.

Local problems in Seattle appeared to be more demanding in the sense that they were less accessible to personal observation. The nature of the most important local problem—unemployment—not only was more salient but required more information and thinking.

The surprising finding was that those with more knowledge did not use media such as television, newspapers, and radio more than did those with less knowledge. The source that correlated most highly with increased knowledge about local problems was personal observation. However, in Seattle there was, in absolute terms, much more use of each of the media than was the case in either Belgrade or Ljubljana. With increased knowledge, respondents in Seattle were more likely to discuss local problems, to attend meetings where problems were discussed, and to want information. But this could be related to the salience of the problem—unemployment.

WORLD PROBLEMS

Belgrade

Those in Belgrade with more knowledge about world problems were more able to suggest more solutions; this had not been the case for local problems. The more knowledgeable individuals also engaged in more media use and communication and used each source of information more than those who had lesser knowledge. They also were more able to evaluate their sources of information critically. In addition, they engaged in the most interpersonal communication, attended more meetings where world problems were discussed, and were most likely to want additional information.

Ljubljana

The pattern observed in Belgrade was observed more distinctively in Ljubljana because of the greater accessibility of external media and higher levels of education. There was an even stronger association of knowledge with decision-making in Ljubljana. There also was a stronger relationship with media use and communication than in Belgrade. This extended to television, radio, press, and personal experience.

In addition, there was a strong association between knowledge and discussion of world problems. However, this did not extend to meetings, which apparently played a lesser function. Nor was knowledge associated with wanting more information about world problems. This was a surprising finding. Evidently, more knowledge was not in itself deemed to be essential.

Seattle

There was a stronger relationship in Seattle between knowledge and the ability to suggest solutions for world problems. Increased knowledge also brought greater media use and communication. Those with more attributes reported more use of television, newspapers, friends, family, and personal experience. Those with the most attributes also were more able to evaluate sources of information.

As contrasted with Belgrade and Ljubljana, there was no association of knowledge of world problems and use of radio. Radio in Seattle had no utility for decision-making.

Those with the most knowledge also discussed problems more with others, participated more in meetings where world problems were discussed, and tended more to want information about world problems. In Seattle, more knowledge was more usable. These results for Seattle differed from what had been observed in Ljubljana.

TABLE 17.1

Belgrade: Number of Problem Attributes on Local Problems as Related to Knowledge and Decision-Making (percentages)

Variable	Number of Problem Attributes			Significance
	0	1	2+	
Number of local problems				.00*
1	48	6	3	
2	16	24	18	
3+	36	70	79	
Number of local solutions				n
0	0	1	0	
1	36	50	46	
2	36	30	30	
3+	28	19	24	
Mentions solution	88	92	94	n

*Significance equals less than .01.

TABLE 17.2

Belgrade: Number of Problem Attributes on Local Problems as Related to Media Use and Communication (percentages)

Variable	Number of Problem Attributes 0	1	2+	Significance
Discussed problem	68	75	81	.08
Attended meeting	24	33	36	n
Wanted more information	52	55	65	.03
Number of sources				n
0	4	3	4	
1	32	25	20	
2	24	18	18	
3+	40	54	59	
Mentioned TV	32	40	42	n
Mentioned radio	20	27	25	n
Mentioned press	52	56	62	.23
Mentioned friend	52	40	51	.01
Mentioned family	4	13	10	n
Mentioned personal experience	84	93	94	.20
Number of source attributes termed most useful				n
0	36	30	31	
1	56	55	56	
2+	8	15	12	
Mentioned useful source attribute	60	69	68	n

TABLE 17.3

Ljubljana: Number of Problem Attributes on Local Problems as Related to Knowledge and Decision-Making (percentages)

	Number of Problem Attributes			
Variable	0	1	2+	Significance
Number of local problems				.00*
1	47	9	2	
2	20	22	15	
3+	34	69	83	
Number of local solutions				.07
0	11	6	2	
1	49	43	40	
2	18	30	39	
3+	21	21	19	
Mentions solution				

*Significance equals less than .01.

TABLE 17.4

Ljubljana: Number of Problem Attributes on Local Problems as Related to Media Use and Communication (percentages)

Variable	Number of Problem Attributes 0	1	2+	Significance
Discussed problem	84	87	92	n
Attended meeting	31	31	39	n
Wanted more information	58	64	62	n
Number of sources				.00*
0	5	1	0	
1	39	35	23	
2	16	12	12	
3+	39	52	65	
Mentioned TV	24	37	40	.08
Mentioned radio	25	30	36	n
Mentioned press	47	51	63	.07
Mentioned friend	27	35	48	.02
Mentioned family	4	10	11	n
Mentioned personal experience	75	94	91	.00*
Number of source attributes termed most useful				.00*
0	56	42	30	
1	30	45	48	
2+	14	13	23	
Mentioned useful source attribute	42	57	71	.00*

*Significance equals less than .01.

TABLE 17.5

Seattle: Number of Problem Attributes on Local Problems as Related to Knowledge and Decision-Making (percentages)

Variable	Number of Problem Attributes				Significance
	0	1	2	3+	
Number of local problems					.00*
1	15	7	2	2	
2	17	17	17	8	
3+	68	76	80	90	
Number of local solutions					.00*
0	21	19	14	8	
1	26	33	29	24	
2	23	29	29	24	
3+	30	19	29	44	
Mentions solution	81	80	86	90	.11

*Significance equals less than .01.

TABLE 17.6

Seattle: Number of Problem Attributes on Local Problems as Related to Media Use and Communication (percentages)

Variable	Number of Problem Attributes 0	1	2	3+	Significance
Discussed problem	93	82	89	91	.03
Attended meeting	21	29	37	39	.04
Wanted more information	49	48	61	60	.02
Number of sources					.00*
0	2	1	1	2	
1	6	9	6	5	
2	30	12	8	6	
3+	62	78	85	87	
Mentioned TV	70	64	63	68	n
Mentioned radio	40	41	39	44	n
Mentioned press	77	76	83	82	n
Mentioned friend	49	51	56	57	n
Mentioned family	21	16	20	23	n
Mentioned personal experience	57	64	68	74	.12
Number of source attributes termed most useful					.00*
0	28	19	12	9	
1	63	63	59	53	
2+	9	18	29	38	
Mentioned useful source attribute	81	84	89	90	.19

*Significance equals less than .01.

TABLE 17.7

Belgrade: Number of Problem Attributes on World Problems as Related to Knowledge and Decision-Making (percentages)

Variable	Number of Problem Attributes 0	1	2+	Significance
Number of world problems				.00*
1	78	16	10	
2	15	33	34	
3+	7	51	56	
Mentions solution	67	88	92	.00*

*Significance equals less than .01.

TABLE 17.8

Belgrade: Number of Problem Attributes on World Problems as Related to Media Use and Communication (percentages)

Variable	Number of Problem Attributes			Significance
	0	1	2+	
Discussed problem	58	75	80	.01
Attended meeting	22	42	38	.02
Wanted more information	33	42	51	.03
Number of sources				.02
0	2	3	1	
1	22	12	6	
2	17	12	12	
3+	59	73	81	
Mentioned TV	63	68	76	.06
Mentioned radio	41	58	61	.05
Mentioned press	78	81	89	.03
Mentioned friend	15	30	34	.04
Mentioned family	9	12	21	.01
Mentioned personal experience	48	46	44	n
Number of source attributes termed most useful				.01
0	22	16	9	
1	65	62	64	
2+	13	22	28	
Mentioned useful source attribute	76	83	90	.01

TABLE 17.9

Ljubljana: Number of Problem Attributes on World Problems as Related to Knowledge and Decision-Making (percentages)

Variable	Number of Problem Attributes 0	1	2+	Significance
Number of world problems				.00*
1	44	9	5	
2	21	25	24	
3+	35	66	71	
Number of world solutions				.00*
0	22	7	3	
1	40	41	29	
2	18	28	42	
3+	20	24	26	
Mentions solution	11	87	90	.00*

*Significance equals less than .01.

TABLE 17.10

Ljubljana: Number of Problem Attributes on World Problems as Related to Media Use and Communication (percentages)

Variable	Number of Problem Attributes			Significance
	0	1	2+	
Discussed problem	75	87	95	.00*
Attended meeting	30	37	35	n
Wanted more information	40	49	50	n
Number of sources				.00*
0	6	1	3	
1	20	10	9	
2	8	6	3	
3+	66	83	85	
Mentioned TV	49	75	77	.00*
Mentioned radio	55	73	71	.01
Mentioned press	77	88	87	.01
Mentioned friend	32	38	36	n
Mentioned family	11	16	11	.21
Personal experience	40	48	61	.01
Number of source attributes termed most useful				.01
0	34	18	16	
1	48	61	58	
2	18	21	26	
Mentioned useful source attribute	69	83	85	.01

*Significance equals less than .01.

TABLE 17.11

Seattle: Number of Problem Attributes on World Problems as Related to Knowledge and Decision-Making (percentages)

	Number of Problem Attributes				
Variable	0	1	2	3+	Significance
Number of world problems					.00*
1	18	6	2	6	
2	20	24	18	8	
3+	63	70	80	85	
Number of world solutions					.00*
0	22	21	13	12	
1	30	37	30	25	
2	28	25	27	23	
3+	20	17	30	40	
Mentions solution	78	79	86	87	.06

*Significance equals less than .01.

TABLE 17.12

Seattle: Number of Problem Attributes on World Problems as Related to Media Use and Communication (percentages)

Variable	Number of Problem Attributes 0	1	2	3+	Significance
Discussed problem	79	79	90	94	.00*
Attended meeting	38	29	41	36	.08
Wanted more information	37	45	56	61	.00*
Number of sources					.03
0	2	4	3	5	
1	11	7	4	3	
2	14	14	9	6	
3+	73	75	84	85	
Mentioned TV	65	69	75	75	.24
Mentioned radio	51	42	49	46	n
Mentioned press	79	75	85	86	.04
Mentioned friend	39	37	51	47	.03
Mentioned family	12	18	19	24	.17
Mentioned personal experience	36	52	51	56	.02
Number of source attributes termed most useful					.00*
0	23	15	10	15	
1	62	71	61	48	
2+	15	13	28	37	
Mentioned useful source attribute	83	90	93	88	.03

*Significance equals less than .01.

CHAPTER

18

THE USES OF MEDIA IN DECISION-MAKING

One frequent criticism of the mass media is that the media constantly portray problems but propose few solutions. The individual is asked to give attention to one important problem after another, most of them beyond his personal competence. The individual thus gains an image of society that is characterized by continuing, unresolvable social problems. Rather than trying to cope with these problems, the individual turns inward and, as a consequence, becomes alienated from mass society. This is the social critic's point of view, and it is widely held.

With respect to at least the first step of that process, our data has lent confirmation to this viewpoint. Our respondents did, in fact, say that they had learned about local and world problems—more significantly the latter—from mass media sources. Given that the media are an important source of knowledge about problems, the question to be answered is whether media use also is associated with an ability on the part of the individual to be aware of solutions to problems.

If greater media use and positive evaluation of media sources of information were associated with having solutions to problems, we could assume that the media also were used instrumentally to that end. A number of questions might subsequently be asked:

1. Were there differences by media? Was it possible, for example, that having solutions to problems was more associated with use of print media and less with use of television and radio?

2. Might media use and efficacy for the individual vary according to the nature of the problem? For example, were there different media effects for local as compared with world problems? Some media might be more useful for local than for world problems, or the inverse might be true. Media have different capacities for presenting certain kinds of events to certain kinds of people.

3. Might media utility for problem-defining and problem-solving vary by culture? That is, might individuals in Belgrade, Ljubljana, and Seattle vary in their use and preferences for media and other communication in relation to decision-making?

We compared individuals who proposed solutions with those who were not able to propose solutions. We asked if having solutions was more, or less, associated with being knowledgeable, using media, using particular media, and using particular modes of evaluating media. Individuals were grouped in terms of the number of solutions they had proposed: no solutions, 1, 2, or 3 or more solutions.

First let us consider the ability of our respondents to cope with local problems.

LOCAL PROBLEMS

Belgrade

In Belgrade, the individuals who had proposed more solutions did, in fact, use more sources of information, and they used newspapers, television, and radio more as sources of information than did those who offered fewer solutions. In addition, family and friends were more used as sources of information by those who offered more solutions.

The most significant differences in behavior were between those who offered no solutions and those who offered a single solution; the differences between those who offered more than one solution and those who offered one solution were not as great. This suggested that media content might be of limited utility to the individual in posing a number of solutions or in helping the individual to cope with a number of solutions; that is, individuals might limit their use of media content to the solution that was most accessible or acceptable to them at a particular time.

In determining whether solution behavior was related to the use of particular media, we found that having a solution was most associated with use of the press, friends, and television. There was some dependence upon radio, although less than upon the press, friends, and television. Family sources, interestingly, were least referred to in relation to solutions.

Ljubljana

The relationship of decision-making to media use was similar in Ljubljana, although it was not as strong. Having solutions again was strongly associated with use of the press, friends, and television. Again, there was less dependence on radio and the family.

An interesting finding was that having any solution in Ljubljana was associated with interpersonal communication, with discussion at meetings, or with wanting more information. The implication was that in Ljubljana people talked more about solutions.

Seattle

There was much greater use of media associated with decision-making in Seattle than in either Belgrade or Ljubljana. Those with more solutions tended to use multiple media, including television, radio, the press, and meetings. This might be due to two factors: 1. The greater absolute use of media across groups. 2. The widespread impact of the local problems in Seattle, i.e., unemployment.

Interestingly, the generally high level of interpersonal discussion in Seattle, as in Ljubljana, was not associated with more effective decision-making. Interpersonal communication presumably did not provide the inputs of information that respondents may have required. Mass media in both cities were more related to decision-making than was interpersonal communication.

In Seattle, as in Ljubljana, differences in decision-making were not related appreciably to attendance at meetings, nor did a broader orientation to decision-making correlate with wanting more information. This suggests that additional information that might have assisted in broader decision-making was not available. Or it might be reasoned that, if any solution had been arrived at, there would be less need for information.

WORLD PROBLEMS

Belgrade

As developed in several of our analyses, world problems tended to require greater use of mass media as sources of information.

In Belgrade, having solutions for world problems was, as we expected, more strongly associated with use of a number of sources of information than was the case for local problems. It was most strongly correlated with use of the press. There also were positive associations with radio, interpersonal communication, and discussion at meetings.

Again it was interesting to note the relationships between having solutions and use of the family as a source of information. The more solutions the individual perceived, the less likely he was to cite his family as a source of information. Nor was having multiple solutions for world problems associated with the viewing of television. Finally, in Belgrade there was no increased association between having multiple solutions and wanting information. This might describe the perceived pertinence of information in the media or the nature of decision-making by the individual. Or, as we proposed, once any decision is made, there might be less need for information.

Ljubljana

In Ljubljana, those with more solutions were more likely to have used more sources of information. The press, again, was the most highly correlated source. Those with more solutions also were more able to point to some personal experience with world problems. And those with more solutions were more likely to have discussed the problems with other persons and at meetings. Thus the nature of world problems, as compared to local problems, apparently made discussion with others increasingly useful to individuals in Ljubljana.

There were even fewer references to the family than in Belgrade, and interestingly there was no significant relationship with respect to personal experience. Also, television was a greater source of information with respect to decision-making in Ljubljana than in Belgrade, very possibly a function of greater access to television sets and Italian and Austrian television.

Seattle

In Seattle, those who had named the most solutions also used more media sources. These included television, the press, and radio, as well as friends, discussion at meetings, and interpersonal communication. However, there were not increasing associations of decision-making with use of radio, friends, family, and personal experience.

Distinctive in Seattle was the tendency by those with solutions to express a need for more information. There was the strongest association here of solution orientation and need for information that we had observed in any of our data. It was possible that the uncertainty relating to the single most important world problem in Seattle—the war in Vietnam—might have demanded a continuing supply of information. Being more informed would not assure the individual that he would, as an individual, be more successful in decision-making, but it would assure knowledge about the changing nature of the decisions that were being made by others.

CONCLUSION

Overall, having solutions to problems was associated with greater media use. Therefore, the conclusion that the media only present problems and do not help individuals to reach decisions did not appear to be justified.

TABLE 18.1

Belgrade: Number of Solutions for Local Problems, as Related to Media Use and Communication (percentages)

Variable	Number of Solutions 0	1	2	3+	Significance
Discussed problem	56	75	81	74	.09
Attended meeting	22	31	34	41	.09
Wanted more information	38	52	62	64	.01
Number of sources for local problems					.02
0	0	2	3	5	
1	56	28	20	19	
2	11	19	18	16	
3+	33	51	59	60	
Mentioned TV	11	37	43	46	.04
Mentioned radio	11	22	29	35	.00*
Mentioned press	44	52	62	64	.00*
Mentioned friend	11	40	47	46	.06
Mentioned family	0	8	16	14	.00*
Mentioned personal experience	100	93	93	92	n
Number of source attributes termed most useful					.01
0	44	35	28	23	
1	56	54	56	58	
2+	0	11	16	19	

*Significance equals less than .01.

TABLE 18.2

Ljubljana: Number of Solutions for Local Problems, as Related to Media Use and Communication (percentages)

Variable	Number of Solutions 0	1	2	3+	Significance
Discussed problem	89	86	88	88	n
Attended meeting	30	28	33	39	.09
Wanted more information	60	60	65	66	n
Number of sources for local problems					.00*
0	15	1	0	1	
1	46	41	24	30	
2	7	14	13	11	
3+	32	45	62	58	
Mentioned TV	24	30	42	41	.01
Mentioned radio	24	26	36	35	.03
Mentioned press	44	41	63	59	.00*
Mentioned friend	22	34	39	40	.15
Mentioned family	7	10	9	9	n
Mentioned personal experience	81	93	91	94	.02
Number of source attributes termed most useful					.00*
0	61	50	30	38	
1	29	40	51	46	
2+	10	10	19	17	

*Significance equals less than .01.

TABLE 18.3

Seattle: Number of Solutions for Local Problems, as Related to Media Use and Communication (percentages)

Variable	Number of Solutions 0	1	2	3+	Significance
Discussed problem	86	86	86	91	n
Attended meeting	17	28	36	43	.00*
Wanted more information	53	51	57	58	n
Number of sources for local problems					.01
0	2	1	1	2	
1	12	7	7	3	
2	19	9	13	8	
3+	67	83	79	88	
Mentioned TV	56	67	63	70	.11
Mentioned radio	26	42	44	45	.01
Mentioned press	67	80	80	86	.00*
Mentioned friend	54	56	46	58	.16
Mentioned family	12	21	22	20	.25
Mentioned personal experience	54	65	71	69	.03
Number of source attributes termed most useful					.00*
0	27	17	15	9	
1	57	61	62	57	
2+	16	23	24	34	

*Significance equals less than .01.

TABLE 18.4

Belgrade: Number of Solutions for World Problems, as Related to Media Use and Communication (percentages)

Variable	Number of Solutions 0	1	2	3+	Significance
Discussed problem	40	72	82	80	.00*
Attended meeting	9	36	47	44	.00*
Wanted more information	36	42	49	44	n
Number of sources for world problems					.05
0	8	3	3	0	
1	8	12	7	15	
2	17	14	9	12	
3+	67	72	81	73	
Mentioned TV	58	71	71	67	n
Mentioned radio	42	56	64	54	.09
Mentioned press	42	83	88	78	.00*
Mentioned friend	42	28	33	32	n
Mentioned family	42	10	17	19	.00*
Mentioned personal experience	67	46	43	45	n
Number of source attributes termed most useful					n
0	25	15	11	17	
1	67	64	63	58	
2+	8	21	26	26	

*Significance equals less than .01.

TABLE 18.5

Ljubljana: Number of Solutions for World Problems, as Related to Media Use and Communication (percentages)

Variable	Number of Solutions 0	1	2	3+	Significance
Discussed problem	71	85	92	89	.00*
Attended meeting	25	33	41	39	.09
Wanted more information	31	46	56	48	.01
Number of sources for world problems					.00*
0	7	1	3	1	
1	21	14	7	7	
2	5	6	6	5	
3+	67	79	84	87	
Mentioned TV	52	73	76	75	.00*
Mentioned radio	57	71	73	72	.12
Mentioned press	67	84	89	94	.00*
Mentioned friend	29	37	38	39	n
Mentioned family	12	16	11	16	n
Mentioned personal experience	50	44	53	54	.14
Number of so source attributes termed most useful					.00*
0	40	23	15	14	
1	41	59	61	63	
2+	19	18	24	24	

*Significance equals less than .01.

TABLE 18.6

Seattle: Number of Solutions for World Problems, as Related to Media Use and Communications (percentages)

Variable	Number of Solutions 0	1	2	3+	Significance
Discussed problem	77	82	84	96	.00*
Attended meeting	21	34	37	47	.00*
Wanted more information	39	50	46	62	.00*
Number of sources for world problems					.01
0	8	4	1	4	
1	10	7	4	3	
2	13	14	12	6	
3+	70	75	83	87	
Mentioned TV	65	67	73	80	.02
Mentioned radio	41	43	54	49	.15
Mentioned press	71	79	86	85	.01
Mentioned friend	43	42	39	52	.12
Mentioned family	22	15	15	22	.18
Mentioned personal experience	55	50	41	53	.08
Number of source attributes termed most useful					.00*
0	24	13	16	10	
1	63	67	60	59	

*Significance equals less than .01.

PART V
MEDIA VARIABLES

CHAPTER

19

COMPLEMENTARINESS OF INFORMATION SOURCES

If media had a complementary influence, those who used the most sources should have a greater knowledge about problems. If media were merely redundant, generally there should be no more knowledge. We thought those would be meaningful hypotheses. Questions as to the consequences of "many media voices" are often raised.

LOCAL PROBLEMS

Belgrade

In Belgrade, there was a progressive relationship between number of sources used and number of local problems named. Not only was this highly significant statistically but the absolute differences were large.

A related question was the extent to which the individual was able to describe the nature of the problem. We defined description as the number of reasons the individual could give for a problem's importance. We found in each case that those who cited more sources could give more information about the problem. We also found a strong association between number of sources used and ability to suggest solutions. Finally, individuals who had more sources of information also wanted additional information. This would suggest that media help to create their own audiences.

Ljubljana

A similar pattern was demonstrated for Ljublana. The greater the number of sources, the greater the tendency to identify and describe local problems and to solve them. There also was the expected relationship between number of sources used and the quality of discriminations made in defining problems and arriving at solutions.

However, individuals in Ljubljana tended to be more active information-seekers than their counterparts in Belgrade. This might be a function of higher levels of education in Ljubljana, as we have indicated previously.

Seattle

As in Belgrade and Ljubljana, there was a progressive relationship in Seattle between number of sources of information and awareness of local problems. There was a similar tendency to be able to propose solutions. Not only were those with more sources of information able to describe problems in more detail—to give more attributes—but they also gave more qualitative attributes.

WORLD PROBLEMS

The most interesting distinction between local and world problems was that, where personal observation sufficed for local problems, mass media sources were needed to gain an understanding of world problems.

Belgrade and Ljubljana

In Belgrade, with respect to solutions, the impact of number of mass media sources was even more evident than for local problems.

The same tendencies were observed in Ljubljana. Those with fewer sources of information were much less aware of world problems.

Similar conditions held with respect to naming more problems, describing those problems more fully, describing them in more qualitative terms, and proposing more solutions. There was a stronger tendency for those with complementary sources to compare problems and to want more information, presumably to maintain levels of awareness.

Seattle

In contrast to Belgrade and Ljubljana, there were no significant variations in Seattle between awareness of local problems and awareness of world problems. This can be explained by our finding that there was a greater tendency to depend upon the media for information about local problems.

CONCLUSIONS

Overall, having multiple sources of information was associated with having knowledge about problems. Knowledge was demonstrated to be more extensive and more qualitative.

There was a great deal of commonality between Belgrade and Ljubljana. But in Seattle, where there was greater dependence upon the media for knowledge about local problems, the contrast with media use for world problems was not as great.

TABLE 19.1

Belgrade: Number of Sources on Local Problems, as Related to Knowledge and Decision-Making (percentages)

Variable	Number of Sources 1	2	3+	Significance
Number of local problems				.00*
1	28	8	4	
2	23	29	16	
3+	49	63	79	
Number of local solutions				.00*
1	64	51	45	
2	21	30	32	
3+	15	19	23	
Compares one problem to another	47	64	59	.00*
Attributes for only one problem	8	13	17	.00*
Problem is important to self	38	41	43	NS

*Significance equals less than .01.

TABLE 19.2

Belgrade: Number of Sources on Local Problems, as Related to Media Use and Communication (percentages)

Variable	Number of Sources 1	2	3+	Significance
Discussed problem	60	79	83	.00*
Attended meeting	28	27	39	.00*
Wanted more information	45	58	64	.00*
Mentioned TV	6	8	67	.00*
Mentioned radio	3	4	45	.00*
Mentioned press	7	39	87	.00*
Mentioned friend	6	46	60	.00*
Mentioned family	1	4	20	.00*
Mentioned personal experience	78	92	92	.00*

*Significance equals less than .01.

TABLE 19.3

Ljubljana: Number of Sources on Local Problems, as Related to Knowledge and Decision-Making (percentages)

Variable	Number of Sources 1	2	3+	Significance
Number of local problems				.00*
1	38	11	8	.00*
2	15	25	20	
3+	47	63	72	
Number of local solutions				.00*
1	71	51	41	
2	16	32	36	
3+	14	17	23	
Compares one problem to another	21	35	34	.00*
Attributes for only one problem	10	16	13	NS
Problem is important to self	39	44	51	.01

*Significance equals less than .01.

TABLE 19.4

Ljubljana: Number of Sources on Local Problems, as Related to Media Use and Communication (percentages)

Variable	Number of Sources 1	2	3+	Significance
Discussed problem	77	90	93	.00*
Attended meeting	27	30	36	.06
Wanted more information	59	65	65	n
Mentioned TV	1	3	67	.00*
Mentioned radio	1	5	57	.00*
Mentioned press	3	38	88	.00*
Mentioned friend	2	48	56	.00*
Mentioned family	0	8	16	.00*
Mentioned personal experience	70	84	94	.00*

*Significance equals less than .01.

TABLE 19.5

Seattle: Number of Sources on Local Problems, as Related to Knowledge and Decision-Making (percentages)

Variable	Number of Sources 1	2	3+	Significance
Number of local problems				.00*
1	48	18	3	
2	7	29	14	
3+	45	53	84	
Number of local solutions				.00*
1	75	49	43	
2	16	32	27	
3+	10	19	31	
Compared one problem to another	10	7	20	.01
Attributes for only one problem	28	37	53	.00*
Problem is important to self	30	43	59	.00*

*Significance equals less than .01.

TABLE 19.6

Seattle: Number of Sources on Local Problems, as Related to Media Use and Communication (percentages)

Variable	Number of Sources 1	2	3+	Significance
Discussed problem	73	69	91	.00*
Attended meeting	16	10	38	.00*
Wanted more information	37	39	59	.00*
Mentioned TV	7	24	76	.00*
Mentioned radio	4	7	49	.00*
Mentioned press	16	57	88	.00*
Mentioned friend	2	35	61	.00*
Mentioned family	0	10	23	.00*
Mentioned personal experience	43	57	67	.00*

*Significance equals less than .01.

TABLE 19.7

Belgrade: Number of Sources on World Problems, as Related to Knowledge and Decision-Making (percentages)

Variable	Number of Sources 1	2	3+	Significance
Number of world problems				.00*
1	63	24	16	
2	17	40	30	
3+	20	36	54	
Number of world solutions				.00*
1	79	59	50	
2	11	22	31	
3+	10	19	18	
Compares one problem to another	23	51	62	.00*
Attributed for only one problem	10	27	29	.00*
Problem is important to self	13	21	19	.12

*Significance equals less than .01.

TABLE 19.8

Belgrade: Number of Sources on World Problems, as Related to Media Use and Communication (percentages)

Variable	Number of Sources			Significance
	1	2	3+	
Discussed problem	63	66	79	.00*
Attended meeting	30	28	44	.00*
Wanted more information	29	43	47	.00*
Mentioned TV	8	40	85	.00*
Mentioned radio	8	22	71	.00*
Mentioned press	15	71	95	.00*
Mentioned friend	4	10	38	.00*
Mentioned family	3	5	17	.00*
Mentioned personal experience	29	40	44	.00*

*Significance equals less than .01.

TABLE 19.9

Ljubljana: Number of Sources on World Problems, as Related to Knowledge and Decision-Making (percentages)

Variable	Number of Sources 1	2	3+	Significance
Number of world problems				.00*
1	62	26	9	
2	14	29	24	
3+	24	45	67	
Number of world solutions				.00*
1	79	48	44	
2	13	31	30	
3+	8	21	26	
Compares one problem to another	24	31	50	.00*
Attributes for only one problem	7	19	19	.00*
Problem is important to self	15	24	26	.01

*Significance equals less than .01.

TABLE 19.10

Ljubljana: Number of Sources on World Problems, as Related to Media Use and Communication (percentages)

Variable	Number of Sources 1	2	3+	Significance
Discussed problem	70	74	91	.00*
Attended meeting	28	14	39	.00*
Wanted more information	33	38	51	.00*
Mentioned TV	8	41	84	.00*
Mentioned radio	4	21	84	.00*
Mentioned press	13	93	96	.00*
Mentioned friend	2	12	44	.00*
Mentioned family	1	0	18	.00*
Mentioned personal experience	33	38	50	.00*

*Significance equals less than .01.

TABLE 19.11

Seattle: Number of Sources on World Problems, as Related to Knowledge and Decision-Making (percentages)

Variable	Number of Sources 1	2	3+	Significance
Number of world problems				.00*
1	43	16	5	
2	17	27	17	
3+	40	57	79	
Number of world solutions				.00*
1	79	57	45	
2	9	28	27	
3+	11	15	28	
Compares one problem to another	17	21	32	.01
Attributes for only one problem	30	49	56	.00*
Problem is important only to self	26	37	37	.18

*Significance equals less than .01.

TABLE 19.12

Seattle: Number of Sources on World Problems, as Related to Media Use and Communication (percentages)

Variable	Number of Sources			Significance
	1	2	3+	
Discussed problem	79	66	89	.00*
Attended meeting	21	22	39	.00*
Wanted more information	36	38	53	.01
Mentioned TV	22	40	80	.00*
Mentioned radio	14	9	55	.00*
Mentioned press	30	54	89	.00*
Mentioned friend	12	21	50	.00*
Mentioned family	9	4	21	.00*
Mentioned personal experience	35	43	50	.03

*Significance equals less than .01.

CHAPTER

20

CREDIBILITY AS A CRITERION

In 1961, Elmer Roper and Associates, under contract to the Television Information Office, began to assess the ways in which publics evaluated their media. These studies generally did not ask respondents to judge media in relation to any particular problem to which their use of media might have been relevant.

Roper asked such questions as the following: Which of the media respondents would "most believe" if they encountered conflicting stories in newspapers, television, magazines, or radio; from which source they got "most of their information" about local and world affairs; and, if they could keep only one of the media, which one they would most wish to keep.

Roper found that during this period television was increasing in credibility while newspapers were becoming less believable. And people increasingly got "most" of their news from television.*

A number of explanations have been offered for this shift in media credibility:

- The "bad news" hypothesis—because newspapers were more given to controversy, they suffered the fate of the messenger who brought bad news. (The broadcast media were somehow apolitical.)

---

*Bush (1966) found that, while such Roper question results could be replicated—specifically, where people get "most" of their "news"—television viewers defined "news" quite narrowly, thinking of "news" as "events." Bush asked those who said they got "most" of their "news" from television why they also read the newspaper. Most of the responses could be categorized as stating that newspaper content had more details and perspective and hence was more characterized as "news"—from that perspective.

- The "creeping liberalism" hypothesis—political bias had infected printed media (but not television).
- The "excellence" hypothesis—the broadcast media were becoming more effective in news presentation and, hence, adequate. (This conclusion was based on the increasing number of people in Roper surveys who said they were getting "most" of their news about local and world affairs, mostly the latter, from television.)

But none of these explanations seems entirely satisfactory. Television has become increasingly controversial in its news presentation. The networks sometimes appear to be more liberal in their commentary than many American newspapers.

If the impact of television is greater than that of the printed media, one should, at the least, expect to encounter as much decrease in the credibility of television as for newspapers. Yet the trend reported by Roper and Associates, corroborated by academic researchers utilizing Roper questions, has not reflected this potential. A number of researchers attempted to cope with this dilemma by carrying out similar studies, but those who used the Roper questions produced similar results.

Carter and Greenberg (1965) approached the problem somewhat differently, concluding that the newspaper press was used more for news and was trusted less, while television was used less for news but trusted more. The investigators contrasted sins of commission by newspapers with sins of omission by television.

Westley and Severin (1964) identified the kinds of individuals who preferred one medium to another, but they used the Roper questions as originally phrased.

Carter and Greenberg revised the Roper question so that it excluded magazines and asked about the credibility of newspapers and magazines without reference to "conflicting" reports. The channel aspects of television permitted, in the judgment of these investigators, a visual dimension that enhanced the believability of "conflicting reports" on television.

Based upon the revised questions, newspapers were judged to be the one source from which respondents got most of their news. However, the Roper findings on credibility were replicated whether the "conflict" element was included or excluded. Even when newspapers were rated for believability in the absence of a contrast with television, they were held to be less believable. The investigators concluded that the comparison with television actually was helpful, rather than odious, as might be the case.

The solution to the dilemma seemed to lie in reconceptualizing source as a mass media variable. The critical question was not whether individuals perceived media images in the abstract but how media sources were relevant when individuals were dealing with a particular problem at a particular time, that is, situationally.

To explain: A media "image" can be thought of as the sum of an individual's prior experience in judging object utilities with that source, over time. But different kinds of problems and situations from time to time should affect an individual's need for and his evaluation of particular media. In practice, individuals should evaluate objects in each situation and find different utilities for different media sources. But the Roper questions forced respondents to cumulate all experience over time and give "object-free" and situationally free responses.

In our research we sought to discover how individuals evaluated media utility in their consideration of specific problems at a specific time. Respondents talked also about media content they themselves had used and the function the media played in helping them to judge particular objects situationally. The objects, as we have been discussing, were local and world problems that the respondents said were personally important to them.

The Roper studies themselves had been attempting to overcome the nonsituational nature of their data. Roper questions were becoming more oriented to specific problems. Questions about sources of information about problems varied topically from "Where do you get most of your news about local and state candidates?" to "Where do you get most of your news about what is going on in the world?" These kinds of questions approached our criterion of situational character, but they lacked two critical elements:

1. The purpose of the "informing" activity: Was the individual merely trying (a) to become aware of the nature of the problem; (b) to define or understand the problem fully; or (c) to solve the problem? How much control was the individual seeking over the object?

2. Conditional factors relating to the nature of the self-informing activity.* Was the problem important or unimportant to the individual, immediate or postponable?

Our purpose was to compare data obtained in a situational setting, where conditions, purposes, and focal objects were specified, with data obtained by the Roper studies in nonsituational settings, where conditions, purposes, and focal objects were not specified.

---

*Another "conditional" factor might be whether or not an issue was controversial as, for example, in political campaigns. Lyle and Stone (1971) demonstrated that "fairness" (which can be translated into credibility) ratings for the media were related to the political preferences of respondents. Other studies, including several by this author, demonstrate that the most critical persons were often the best informed; hence, the amount and quality of knowledge held by the individual might be another criterion in conceptualization.

FINDINGS

In each of our three cultures, whether local or world problems, the press, not television, was most often reported as a source of information. The same order of utility—press, television, and then radio—was observed in each setting.

We also asked our respondents where they got most of their information about their problems. The media were ranked again in the order of press, television, and radio. More significantly, we asked respondents where they got their most useful information.

The press again was cited in this case as the most useful source in all three cultures. The press was the most employed for local problems. Television more closely approximated newspapers as a most useful source of information about world problems.

We asked also about least useful sources of information. Newspapers in relative terms were less often named least useful than television or radio. This was most noticeable with respect to local news—where the press was most dominant—but it was true as well for world problems.

What criteria did individuals use to evaluate their sources of information? The traditions of media "image" research, popularized by Roper, had focused attention upon credibility. Were there more relevant criteria?

Individuals who named two or more sources of information were asked, "Which source was most useful?" and "Why?" The distribution of responses to the evaluative question confirms the suspicion that source credibility was not the most critical variable for the individual; content, availability, and channel dimensionalities were of far greater significance.

In all three cultures, cognitive and availability criteria were dominant, not only for important local problems but also for important world problems.

(Responses coded as "cognitive" included references to completeness, detail, integration, comprehension, and so forth. Responses coded as "availability" included statements that the person was available to the source or it was available to him; this extended to pragmatic responses such as "I'm there" and "It's there." Channel dimensionality statements said essentially that the medium was the message—you can see it, read it at your leisure, and so forth. Responses coded as "trustworthiness" or "credibility" included references to trust and dependence; we looked for "source" or "content" referents in making a decision where the term "reliability" was used. It is evident that reliability is also a component of cognition, but it appears to be more implicit than explicit. A content reference defined it as a "cognitive" response.)

Perhaps the most interesting aspect of trustworthiness or credibility was in its positive and negative contexts. Trustworthiness appeared to be more of a negative than a positive criterion; that is to say, lack of trustworthiness appeared a better reason for not using a source than trustworthiness was for using a source.

Our final question concerned how the media were evaluated. Which medium would be most trusted? Most characterized by cognitive criteria, accessibility, or channel dimensionalities?

In Belgrade, for local and world problems, radio was most characterized by accessibility, the press by cognitive, and television by channel dimensionalities. These characterizations were even more dramatic with respect to world news.

Ljubljana followed the same pattern, but the channel characteristics of television were not mentioned as frequently. Ljubljana's position in relation to the other European broadcasting centers—notably in Austria and Italy—made radio more valuable because of its availability. Relevant to this was a higher score for cognitive dimensionalities for radio.

In Seattle, cognitive criteria were cited more for all media. The emphasis television placed on local news produced cognitive responses. By contrast, there were few references to cognitions for radio about world problems. Bulletins about world news contributed awareness, but little knowledge.

Overall, the data from the three cities indicated that, when individuals were permitted to describe problems that were important to them, newspapers were mentioned most often as sources of information about those problems. Television was the second most useful mass media source.

The credibility or trustworthiness criterion did not seem too elevant to the individual at the point of evaluating information the individual was using situationally in problem-definition and decision-making. More relevant to the individual was the content of the media—that is, cognitive consideration, accessibility or convenience of the media, and channel dimensionalities.

These findings must be interpreted in terms of the conditions that were specified:

1. Individuals were coping with problems important to them, personally.

2. They were engaged in problem-definition and decision-making.

3. The focal objects—a problem in the local community and a problem in the world community—gave a highly situational character to the process.

We can conclude, at best, that the Roper findings are highly limited in their applications. Their findings are essentially attitudinal rather than situational. A reassessment of the Roper methodology might be justified by our findings.

PART VI
EVALUATION

CHAPTER

21

PROFILE OF THE MODEL

The research design posed two major sets of predictive variables: (1) social characteristics—education, sex, and income; and (2) cognitive characteristics—the number of problems and solutions in the respondents' cognitive fields and the extent to which they could describe the importance of those problems by various kinds of attributes.

Our multiple regression analysis combined these two groups of variables into one set of predictors. We looked first at the extent to which each variable correlated with the other, and then at the cumulated variance. This told us the extent to which each variable served as a predictor of probable use of multiple sources of information, and the cumulative predictive value of all the variables.

BELGRADE

Local Problems

In Belgrade the number of sources of information about local problems was most positively correlated with the number of local problems mentioned by the individual, and with being a male rather than a female. There were low correlations with the amount of knowledge about the local problems, higher income, and having a university education.

But, curiously, a greater incidence of solutions does not accompany a greater number of problems in Belgrade. Further, the use of multiple sources of information was not correlated with having solutions—only with knowledge.

Thus, knowing about problems is aided by use of information sources, but information sources do not help the individual to know how to cope with that problem. These are provocative findings for local problems in Belgrade, consistent with our previous observations but providing perspective.*

World Problems

It is interesting to compare our findings about use of multiple sources of information on local problems with that for world problems. Here, the emphasis varies and more behavior can be predicted. This means that multiple sources of information are more important for a better understanding of world problems than for local problems in Belgrade.

Having knowledge about world problems is strongly correlated with use of multiple sources of information. Only the number of world problems perceived by the individual, and a primary level of education, are stronger predictors. However, having solutions for world problems is negatively correlated with use of multiple sources of information.

Lest this seem too strange, it should be remembered that the most important source of information in Belgrade was personal experience, both for world and for local problems. It should also be remembered that the "information" used to solve problems at times appeared to be related not to contemporary but to past problems, for which new information apparently was not perceived as being relevant. Hence, media were less relevant. In this respect, Belgrade was unlike both Ljubljana and Seattle. Naming more problems did not mean naming more solutions. There was, in fact, a curious tendency for women, those of low education, and those who were least informed about problems to be aware of more solutions to world problems. Referring to our earlier findings that these groups used less sophisticated problem attributes, the inference can be made that the nature of the solutions might also be unsophisticated and based on what we call trans-situational attributes.

To explain: Trans-situational attributes are those that have been used to judge objects that also possessed different attributes. They reflect the tendency to judge the different objects as being similar. Some subjects merely revived a problem with which they were familiar in the past. It would not be inappropriate for us to speculate that there might have been more references to earlier world problems

---

*Total variance explained was 7 percent.

in Belgrade than in Ljubljana. One would not require "new" information to cope with "old" problems.

Looking at our predictive variables, we can see some implications of this discussion. First, the number of world problems was the best predictor of use of number of information sources, followed by primary level of education and seniority in age. This would be a startling outcome for "new" problems. Thus, apparently our older, less educated respondents were the ones who remembered and revived earlier world problems.

A second set of influences then came into play: more knowledge of world problems—that is, number of attributes, number of solutions, level of income, and a university level of education—for a second group of individuals oriented to contemporary world problems: the young and the educated, and the informed. This suggests the need for a factor analytic approach by which these types of individuals might be more clearly and fully identified.

Overall, rather than only 7 percent of the variance being explained, as for local problems, some 10 percent was explained for world problems. This meant that multiple sources of information were more essential for world problems than for local problems.

LJUBLJANA

Local Problems

Apparently, there were fewer idiosyncratic influences at work in Ljubljana on local problems. For example, number of sources of information was most highly correlated with number of problems, with reasons why problems were important, and with number of solutions proposed for problems. These findings closely reflected the assumptions implicit in our research design.

Number of sources of information also was positively correlated with extent of income and, to a limited extent, with having a university education.

Turning to negative associations, number of sources of information was most negatively correlated with having only an elementary school education, with being in the oldest age group, and having only a secondary level of education. There was a very small negative correlation with being a female. These findings, too, fit our model.

Looking at our power to predict use of multiple sources of information, the number of local problems was the strongest predictor. This was followed by the number of problem attributes (rather than by the age of the respondent, as in Belgrade), then by age, number of solutions, education, and male or female role. As in Belgrade, only 7 percent of the variance was explained by the nine variables. However, the nature of the contribution of each variable varied a great deal between the two cities.

World Problems

The picture with respect to world problems in Ljubljana differed considerably from what was reflected for local problems. Number of sources of information about world problems was highly correlated with the number of problems observed. Significant relationships also were present with respect to level of income and a university level of education.

There was a significant relationship, as well, to having attributes for problems, but only slight relationships with male and female roles and with having solutions for problems. It is interesting that again media were not strongly related to awareness of a greater number of solutions to problems. Presumably, the solutions again were "old" ones, or new solutions were not being proposed in the media at that time.

Interestingly, having solutions was correlated most strongly with having knowledge about the problems, and was actually slightly negatively related to levels of education. Thus, knowledge more than education was related to awareness of solutions to world problems—again an interesting finding.

With respect to prediction, tendencies were stronger and somewhat more variance was explained, a total of 13 percent. The best prediction of multiple media usage was explained by the number of world problems proposed by the respondents.

SEATTLE

Local Problems

Use of multiple sources of information about local problems is for the first time a function of local problems as well as solutions. The Seattle media apparently contributed not only to an awareness of problems but also to an awareness of solutions. Knowledge about why local problems were important was in turn correlated with use of multiple sources of information.

The other significant relationship with multiple sources of information was university level of education. This relationship was modest, although stronger than in Belgrade and Ljubljana. As we pointed out earlier, local problems in Seattle appear to be less "local" than in the Yugoslav cities. Apparently, fewer local problems in Seattle were susceptible to personal observation; thus, they were more subject to media inputs than in Belgrade and Ljubljana.

Older people and the least well educated used markedly fewer sources of information. There were no significant differences in terms of sex roles or income.

Being aware of solutions was strongly related to number of problems, an ability to give reasons for the importance of problems, and having a university education. Again there were only minor relationships with male and female roles, although men were less attuned to local problems than were women. Those of lower education also were less attuned to local problems. It would seem that persons of lower income and education did not participate broadly in local affairs.

Looking at the predictive power of each of the variables, use of many sources of information was best predicted by the number of solutions and problems that a person had under surveillance. Age was the next most reliable predictor, followed by knowledge of the importance of problems. The other variables contributed significantly less to the prediction.

Overall, the Seattle data showed a stronger cognitive component to prediction of multiple media use than in Ljubljana, and markedly stronger than in Belgrade, where knowledge of problems and solutions did not predict use of multiple sources of information. In Belgrade, particularly, there was a dependence upon the individual's observation—and, undoubtedly, personal involvement with the problem.

World Problems

In Seattle, it was evident from looking at the correlation matrix that use of multiple sources of information was most highly correlated with the number of world problems perceived by the individual. But, contrary to Belgrade and Ljubljana, multiple media use also was highly correlated with the number of solutions. This was a distinctive difference, suggesting that media were more depended upon for solutions to world problems.

Use of multiple sources of information also was significantly correlated with knowing why the problem was important, but only modestly with a university level of education.

Significantly negative correlations were found with age and with having only a primary level of education. These in turn were highly correlated; that is, most of the oldest respondents in the Seattle sample had only a primary level of education.

There was a very strong relationship between number of problems and number of solutions, suggesting that in Seattle people who permit themselves to become cognizant of a large number of problems may do so because they are capable of learning about solutions to those problems.

Turning to the amount and source of variance explained, the variations from Belgrade and Ljubljana are of interest. Most of the use of multiple sources of information could be predicted by the number of solutions a person could propose for world problems. Stated another way, those who were considering the most solutions to a problem tended to use more sources of information about those problems. Another major reason for use of information was the number of problems being considered by the individuals. The other variables contributed small amounts to a total variance explained of 12.4 percent.

CHAPTER

22

PROFILES OF THE PERSONS INTERVIEWED

Our questionnaire yielded what in many cases were intimate portraits of the respondents. They had told us what they perceived as their problems, some solutions to those problems, and their sources of information and advice. It was necessary to group these individuals and their responses to get a view of the collectivities. But our methodological approach permitted us to portray the profiles of individuals, as well.

These individual profiles could give us a feeling for the validity of groupings. How well did individuals fit the group patterns that had emerged from our analysis? Was education, for example, an invariate predictor of individual behavior? Probably not, for no variable governs all our behavior. Some respondents would fit patterns, but others would vary from them. In what ways?, we wondered. And how did our predictive variables interact with one another to account for the communication and decision-making behaviors we had sought to observe? How predictive were our variables at the level of the individual?

EDUCATION

Education did assert itself in the case of a 67-year-old Belgrade woman who was widowed and living alone on a small pension. In terms of her age and the fact that she was no longer employed, she could easily have lost a sense of involvement in community and world problems. But a university level education apparently helped her to maintain an ability to participate meaningfully.

She mentioned many local problems and sources of information about them, and she had discussed the problems with others. She had not participated in meetings, but this was understandable in view of her age and isolation.

She was sophisticated in both her reference to media and her means of evaluating them: For example, her most useful source of information was the press, and the least useful was television. She preferred the press because of its content. While she mentioned only one world problem, she showed a strong pattern of media use and discrimination. More extensive and discriminating use of media should be an expected corollary of education, but it was all the more remarkable in this elderly woman.

We looked, by contrast, at a 45-year-old Ljubljana woman of very modest education and income who was employed as a laborer. She named only one problem and could say only that it was important to her personally. While she could offer a solution, she could not mention any solutions named by others. Her only source of knowledge was personal experience, nor did she want more information.

Her outlook was much the same for world problems. She referred only to personal experience and to discussions with others. Her picture was one of limited orientation due to lower education, income, and social role. She could not surpass her role because she lacked the mobility provided by education.

A different picture was present in a 56-year-old Seattle engineer of college education who was highly informed and oriented to local and world problems and their solutions. But, while his media use was extensive, his ways of evaluating media were not discriminating. Thus, education was not a thoroughly reliable predictor in his case.

He said television was his most useful source of information for both local and world problems because of its convenience, not because of its content. He could not rely upon his friends for information about world problems, he said, because they did not have dependable information. He appeared to expect a great deal of his friends. Higher education would have predicted more sophisticated bases for evaluation of information sources—and for choices of sources. Thus, education itself was not a sufficient predictor of behavior.

SEX ROLES

Some effects of sex roles were illustrated by a 45-year-old married Belgrade woman of secondary school, humanistic education. She was in a higher income grouping, but was herself employed as a clerk. She named several local problems but did not propose many solutions for them. Although she named five sources of information, including television and the press, meetings were more useful to her than any of her other sources. She said she found experts there.

Her orientation to world problems was constrained. She named only one problem and two sources—the press and personal experience. The press was her most useful source because she trusted it the most, not because of any specific content. She did not want additional information. This fitted the finding that she was not strongly oriented to decision-making.

Her pattern was one of modest media use and nondiscriminating evaluation of media. Despite her higher level of education, she was not attuned to decision-making. A woman's role appeared to constrict the use of her other attributes.

This behavior contrasted with that of a single, 44-year-old Belgrade woman of college education and middle income who held an administrative job. Her education and profession emancipated her from the confining aspects of a woman's role. She was quite knowledgeable about local problems. She described them, compared them, and also noted her own involvement. But she named only two sources of information—friends and personal experience. She had discussed the problems with her peers and at meetings. She said she had enough information.

She obviously was not media-oriented. Her personal experience was most useful in making decisions about local problems, she said, because she could observe for herself. In other individuals, this could be seen as confining. In her case, given professional and educational mobility, it appeared to be more discriminating than isolating.

This could be observed with respect to world problems. Here she was also very knowledgeable but again excluded the mass media as sources of information. Books were the source of most of her information. They were most useful because they were most relevant, she said, while friends were least dependable.

The sex role also was minimized in the case of a 42-year-old Ljubljana woman with a secondary school education and a fairly high level of income. She was well informed about local problems, could provide solutions for them, and cited press and television as sources of information. Her most useful source was the press because it was most competent and had the most information. Her least important source was television because it lacked completeness of presentation. These were sophisticated, content-relevant responses.

She maintained her orientation to media with respect to world problems, and again named the press as most useful because of its content. Radio was least useful because she listened to it so seldom. But it was interesting that she could suggest no solutions to world problems.

Quite clearly, education and income in her case created a more profound orientation to media, but a woman's role was implied in her inability to propose solutions to world problems

A Seattle woman discussed a range of problems and also used a variety of media, particularly for world problems, but she did not evaluate media in a qualitative way. She said radio was her most useful source of information about local problems because it contained the most complete reports. This was an unusual characterization of radio news. Radio, she said, also was most useful to her as a source of information about world problems. But this time the reason was the convenience and accessibility of radio, a more understandable response. Curiously, she added that the press provided the least information.

This woman, uninformed and unable to cope with media or decision-making, appeared to be representative of a constrained sex role.

Looking at our profiles, men were more oriented to world problems and women to local problems. That also was suggestive of role. Two cases were illustrative. A Belgrade woman named many local problems and cited the radio, press, personal observation, and discussion with others as sources of information. She mentioned only two world problems and was unable to name solutions. A Seattle man, by contrast, named numerous world problems and proposed more solutions for them than for local problems. And he cited more sources of knowledge about world problems than for local problems.

Men also were more attuned to decision-making, but quality of decision-making was not always more evident. There was the suggestion in some of our profiles that men made decisions on less adequate grounds than women did.

A 56-year-old Seattle college graduate is illustrative. He mentioned numerous local and world problems and used media extensively. He proposed several solutions for local and world problems. But the quality of his decision-making was questionable. Television was his most useful source of information about local problems because it happened to be "on" at a time convenient to him each day. The press was his most useful source of information about world problems because there was a newspaper in the house and he read it each day. In neither case did he mention anything he had seen or read about the problem.

AGE

Age, like sex, proved in our collective analysis to be a confining role. This was particularly the case among the elderly of low education, affecting men as well as women.

A 65-year-old Belgrade man was a college graduate and living on his pension. His educational competencies helped him to maintain contact with problems through the media. But people, he said, were his most useful source of information about local problems because they knew personally about the events, while television was his most useful source of information about world problems because it enabled one to see what was actually happening. Television and people "took him where he needed to be."

The confining impact of age also was illustrated in the case of a 69-year-old Ljubljana worker of low education. He was interested in several local problems and mentioned several sources of information about them, including television and the press, and he could propose solutions for those problems. However, his most useful source of information was television. The reason again was that "one could see the event" on television. His educational limitations were expressed when he said that the press was least useful to him because it required so much effort to get the information. However, his most useful source of information about world problems was the press, but the reason was that he could trust it more than he could trust his friends. He did not cite any attributes of the world problem; he was going on trust, not on knowledge. His isolation—a function of age—had increased his dependency on other people.

A 65-year-old Seattle woman, a retired nurse, had less than a high school education. She relied most on personal experience because, she said, she could depend upon her own observations. She was apparently unable to use media effectively. The press, she said, did not have the information she needed to cope with local problems.

She experienced even greater difficulties with world problems. Her sources of information were extensive, but again she experienced difficulty in using media. Radio was most useful because it was "on all the time." She obviously was unable to discriminate very meaningfully among the functions and utilities of media.

One of the most evident pictures of isolation associated with age—in this case representing a lack of access to media—was that of a 73-year-old Belgrade woman. She was retired and single and lived alone. Although her income was moderate and her education was higher than the average, she could name only one local problem, had not discussed the problem with others, and said she did not want any additional information.

In her case, the effects of education were not enough to maintain contact with the outside world. Age was the source of attrition of her educationally derived capabilities.

Our analysis of age groupings had shown limitation in our youngest groups as well. A 23-year-old Ljubljana woman who was very knowledgeable about local and world problems also named an unusually large number of sources of information about them. But she was not attuned to decision-making. She could not refer to any solutions to local problems proposed by others. And she had no solutions herself for any world problems.

A 28-year-old Seattle chemist with a university education mentioned numerous local and world problems, and the press and television among other sources of information, but he did not want more information about the problems nor was he oriented to decision-making. The press was his most useful source of information, but it was because the press "was available" or "for no reason." He did not demonstrate the ability to evaluate media sources that a college education might suggest.

INCOME

In regard to income, we expected to see patterns of media use and decision-making that were observed among educational groupings. But income demonstrated some of its own effects.

A 51-year-old Belgrade man, a laborer, was one of our highest income respondents, but his income did not compensate for a lack of education. He named only two local problems and was able to describe them only to a limited extent. This was not surprising, for he cited only one source of information—personal experience. He had not discussed the problems with others or at meetings. He said only that the problem was important to him, personally. While he had a solution for the problem, he could not suggest solutions proposed by others.

No world problems were important to him. Thus, despite a high income, his behavior was characterized by a lack of media use, a reliance on personal experience, and a highly constricted orientation to problems. This was explained by low occupational status and level of education.

A 40-year-old divorced woman in Ljubljana, also of low income and education and employed as a laborer, named several local problems and provided a solution for her most important problem, but she could not mention solutions proposed by others. She said her most useful source of information was television because it contained the most information. Least useful was the press, because of its content. These were indiscriminate responses. Her world problems profile was similar. Television again was her most useful source of information, while the press was least useful.

Limitations of income and education limited her ability to cope with solutions to problems. And her modes for evaluating media were, as we have seen, not appropriate to the media she cited.

NUMBER OF SOURCES OF INFORMATION

We looked finally at profiles of our respondents in terms of number of sources of information. The profiles again were revealing.

A 24-year-old Ljubljana woman had utilized media widely for world problems, and she was content-oriented. But she had only a primary school education, was employed as a clerk, and was of low income. The media provided her with knowledge about world problems, but her limitations in education and constricted social role limited the ways she could use media effectively.

By contrast, a 26-year-old Seattle teacher was strongly oriented to media and also to decision-making. He cited six sources of information about world problems, including all of the media, and he proposed six possible solutions to the problems. The combined factors of education, male role, and media use thus were highly predictive in his case.

An exception to our collective analysis of media impact was a 65-year-old Belgrade woman. She had only a primary level education and was living alone on a small income. Although she cited all media as sources of information about world problems, she actually could name only one world problem she gave no information about it, and she could not cite solutions proposed by others. Media, in her case, were not enough. She was constricted by age and level of education.

CONCLUSION

Overall, we were satisfied that the individual profiles illustrated the validity of the collective analysis and also pointed to the variation and complexity of the behavior implicit in it.

CHAPTER

23

CONCLUSIONS AND EVALUATION

This research has proposed a number of new approaches to the study of mass communication. Because the research is innovative in many respects—in its conceptualization of variables, in its methodological approach, and in its crosscultural context—it is difficult to sum up and evaluate the findings in a single chapter. Therefore, the effort here will be directed toward highlighting aspects of the research that deserve restatement and pointing to implications of findings that may have escaped the reader's attention.

It is evident that the focus of the research is upon problem definition and problem-solving in the context of mass communication. What is significant about the approach is that it takes the point of view of the individual who is attempting to cope with problems he defines for himself. He deals with a problem as it affects him at a particular time. He is thus defining a situation in his own terms. This is what we call a situational approach.

In attitudinal research, as contrasted to our situational approach, the individual is required to cope with "classes" of problems proposed by an investigator. The means of coping with these problems also are suggested by the investigator. Time and place and event are merged so that behaviors take on a general rather than a specific character. Individuals cumulate their experience and judge their behavior over time rather than observing it at one point in time. They judge with respect to a class of events rather than a particular event. Thus the attitudinal approach is critically different in conceptualization and methodology from the research represented by this study.

A situational approach has permitted actual mass communication behaviors to emerge. These behaviors have been expressed by new variables. These have included knowledge and decision-making about local and world problems, and media use and evaluation related to these problems.

Our data show support for the principle that the audiences for mass communication are selective in their needs and capacities to use information. Not all of the audiences for mass communication view themselves as decision-makers. A purpose of this research has been to identify audience behaviors and, by inference, their needs.

Our data have shown that individuals with different capacities to use information use different media for that information. Social criteria such as age, education, sex role, and income role are predictive of some communication behaviors.

Communication needs also are expressed in the various cognitive styles that were evidenced. Individuals who were aware of more problems, who were able to define those problems in more sophisticated ways, and who were able to solve those problems in their own minds, tended more to use all media. They cited print media rather than television as most useful to them. Few mentioned radio as compatible with their more sophisticated needs.

Some of these findings challenged previous research reported in both Yugoslavia and the United States. One reason for these variations in findings was apparent. We were asking individuals about important problems: How did the individual use sources of information to cope with this particular problem at this particular time? We did not ask about classes of problems over time; the latter question would be attitudinal.

When we asked individuals to tell us why their sources of information were more or less useful to them, we found that they did not invoke the same criteria that had been imposed upon respondents in often repeated earlier studies. They did not cite media credibility as their most important criterion; they more often cited such factors as the content of the message, the availability and accessibility of the source of information, or the special characteristics of that channel of information—that is, in McLuhan's terms, the medium was the message.

While our research design was unique in its methodology and situational character, of equal importance was the crosscultural dimension. We could not intelligently compare individuals across cultures unless there were bases for comparison. Our research, therefore, sought to establish common grounds for comparing individuals in different cultures. We began by reasoning that, if individuals were equally concerned about problems, we could compare their behaviors with respect to those "equivalent" problems. Whatever the culture, we assumed, individuals defined problems in some ways. We therefore gave our respondents the opportunity to state why the problems thay had defined as most important (to them) had gained this importance. We found that modes of problem definition also lent themselves to comparison.

We further articulated our research design, presented earlier, to compare individuals who were equivalent in their social characteristics with respect to their use and evaluation of sources of information and advice. The data were internally consistent; that is, the responses correlated in expected ways.

The question occurs to us, of course, as to the generalizability of our data. Is one situation equivalent to another situation? How many situations must we explore to move toward the development of theory in mass communication?

Actually, we permitted our respondents to talk about two situations—about one local and one world problem. Respondents discriminated significantly in their cognitive and communications behavior with respect to each focal object. And when we cumulated media behavior across two focal objects, the media exposure scores began to approximate the total exposure that is produced by attitudinal studies.

It is our view that it is easier to generalize about what we observe than to infer what happens in specific situations from attitudinal data. This proposes that a number of situational studies, spaced out over time and working with a variety of specific problems, can give us a basis for theory in mass communication.

Attitudinal studies in the past may have obscured mass communication behavior. In presenting the respondent with a statement or an assertion, the social scientist has provided object, attribute, and even context. Respondents have not been required to describe or compare, nor have they been permitted to provide pertinent attributes. The social scientist has done the thinking for his audiences.

Our methodological approach is, in this sense, journalistic and humanistic. It is journalistic in its development of a point of view; it is humanistic in taking the point of view of the individual who is coping with the problem or event.

This study represents only a partial analysis of a rich store of data. There are additional opportunities for analyses. We may go on to abstract audience, content, and media typologies. And we might wish to look more intensively at more subtle effects.

The cross cultural perspectives, above all, must be kept in view. This is the only study of its kind where a socialist and a captialist media system have been compared directly at the community level on their utilities for the individual. Whatever the deficiencies in conceptualization or analysis, this may be considered, we hope, as a landmark work.

APPENDIX A

QUESTIONNAIRE

1. Are there any problems facing the city of (Belgrade) (Ljubljana) (Seattle)?

   ☐ Yes. Go to Question 2.
   ☐ No. Go to Question 18.

2. What are those problems?

   ☐ ____________________
   ☐ ____________________
   ☐ ____________________
   ☐ ____________________

   Probe: What are some other problems facing (Belgrade) (Ljubljana) (Seattle)?

   ☐ ____________________
   ☐ ____________________
   ☐ ____________________

3. Which of these problems is the most important to you personally?

   ☐ ____________________

   If the respondent cannot name the "most important problem," say: "Well, let's take the first problem you mentioned, ____. How long have you been aware of the problem of ____?"

   ☐ ____________________

   Then: Go to Question 5.

4. Why is that problem more important to you than the other problems you have mentioned?

☐ ______

☐ ______

☐ ______

Probe: Are there any other reasons why this problem is more important to you than the other problems you have mentioned?

☐ ______

☐ ______

4A. How long have you been aware of this problem?

☐ ______

5. How did you learn about this problem?

☐ ______

☐ ______

☐ ______

If "press" or "newspapers,"
ask: "From which newspaper?"

☐ ______

If "radio,"
ask: "From which station? Program?"

☐ ______

If "television,"
ask: "From which program?"

☐ ______

Probe: Did you learn about this problem in any other ways?

☐ ______

☐ ______

If "press" or "newspaper,"
ask: "From which newspaper?"

☐ ____________________

If "radio,"
ask: "From which station? Program?"

☐ ____________________

If "television,"
ask: "From which program?"

☐ ____________________

6. Have you discussed this problem with anyone?

☐ Yes
☐ No
☐ Don't know

7. Has this problem been discussed at any meeting that you have attended?

☐ Yes
☐ No
☐ Don't know

8. Do you want more information about this problem?

☐ Yes. Go to Question 8A.
☐ No } Go to Question 9.
☐ Don't know } Go to Question 9.

8A. What kind of information would you like to have?

☐ ____________________
☐ ____________________
☐ ____________________

Probe: What other information would you like to have about this problem?

☐ ____________________

☐ ____________________

9. Now let me ask you about another aspect of __________. What should be done to solve the problem of __________?

☐ ____________________

☐ ____________________

☐ ____________________

If respondent says "don't know," ask: "What solutions have been proposed?"

☐ ____________________

☐ ____________________

☐ ____________________

Then: Go to Question 10.

9A. What other solutions have been proposed?

☐ ____________________

☐ ____________________

☐ ____________________

☐ ____________________

If respondent provides no "other solutions," then: Go to Question 10.

9B. Why do you prefer __________ to the other solution(s) you mentioned?

☐ ____________________

☐ ____________________

☐ ____________________

Probe: Any other reasons why you prefer ________ to the other solution(s) you have mentioned?

☐ ____________________

☐ ____________________

Give the respondent the list of sources of information about the (Belgrade) (Ljubljana) (Seattle) problem that was most important to him.

On this piece of paper we have circled the sources of information about the problem of ________ that you mentioned. We would like to ask you a few questions about these sources. Please answer only with those sources that have been circled.

10. From what sources have you received the most useful information about the problem of ______________?

☐ ____

10A. Why compared to the other sources you have mentioned, was __________ the most useful?

☐ ____

☐ ____

☐ ____

11. From what source have you received the least useful information about the problem of _____________?

☐ ____

11A. Why compared to the other sources you have mentioned, was __________ the least useful?

☐ ____

☐ ____

☐ ____

12. From which of these sources have you received the most information about the problem of _____________?

☐ ____

13. From what source have you received the least information about the problem of ______________?

☐ ____

14. From what source have you received the most trustworthy information about the problem of ______________?

☐ ____

15. From what source have you received the least trustworthy information about the problem of ____________?

☐ ____

If the respondent said "don't know" to Question 9: "What should be done to solve the problem of ____________?" do not ask him Questions 16 and 17. Go to Question 18.

16. Which source helped you most to determine the solutions to the problem of ____________?

☐ ____

17. Which source helped you the least to determine the solutions to the problem of ____________?

☐ ____

18. We'd like to turn now to another subject and ask you a few more questions. Are there any problems facing the world today?

☐ Yes. Go to Question 19.
☐ No. Go to Question 35.

19. What are those problems?

☐ ____
☐ ____
☐ ____
☐ ____

Probe: What are some other problems facing the world today?

☐ ____
☐ ____
☐ ____

20. Which of these world problems is the most important to you personally?

☐ ____

If the respondent cannot name the "most important problem,"
say: "Well, let's take the first problem you mentioned, ________.

How long have you been aware of the world problem of ________?

☐ ____

Then: Go to Question 22.

21. Why is that world problem more important to you than the other world problems that you have mentioned?

☐ ____

☐ ____

☐ ____

Probe: Are there any other reasons why this world problem is more important to you than the other world problems you have mentioned?

☐ ____

☐ ____

21A. How long have you been aware of this problem?

☐ ____

22. How did you learn about this world problem?

☐ ____

☐ ____

☐ ____

If "press" or "newspapers,"
ask: "From which newspaper?"

☐ ____

If "radio,"
ask: "From which station? Program?"

☐ ____

If "television,"
ask: "From which program?"

☐ ____________________

Probe: Did you learn about this world problem in any other ways?

☐ ____________________

☐ ____________________

If "press" or "newspapers,"
ask: "From which newspaper?"

☐ ____________________

If "radio,"
ask: "From which station? Program?"

☐ ____________________

If "television,"
ask: "From which program?"

☐ ____________________

23. Have you discussed this world problem with anyone?

☐ Yes
☐ No
☐ Don't know

24. Has this world problem been discussed at any meeting that you have attended?

☐ Yes
☐ No
☐ Don't know

25. Do you want more information about this world problem?

☐ Yes. Go to Question 25A.
☐ No } Go to Question 26.
☐ Don't know }

25A. What kind of information would you like to have?

☐ ______________________________

☐ ______________________________

☐ ______________________________

Probe: What other information would you like to know?

☐ ______________________________

☐ ______________________________

26. Now let me ask you about another aspect of the world problem of ________.
What should be done to solve the world problem of ________?

☐ ______________________________

☐ ______________________________

☐ ______________________________

If respondent says "don't know,"
ask: "What solutions have been proposed?"

☐ ______________________________

☐ ______________________________

☐ ______________________________

Then: Go to Question 27.

26A. What other solutions have been proposed?

☐ ______________________________

☐ ______________________________

☐ ______________________________

☐ ______________________________

If the respondent provides no "other solutions,"
Then: Go to Question 27.

26B. Why do you prefer ___________ to the other solution(s) you have mentioned?

☐ ____

☐ ____

☐ ____

Probe: Any other reasons why you prefer _________ to the other solution(s) you have mentioned?

☐ ____

☐ ____

Give the respondent the list of sources of information about the world problem that was most important to him.

On this piece of paper we have circled the sources of information about the world problem of _________ that you mentioned. We would like to ask you a few questions about these sources. Please answer only with those sources that have been circled.

27. From what sources have you received the most useful information about the world problem of ____________?

☐ ____

27A. Why, compared to the other sources you have mentioned, was ____________ the most useful?

☐ ____

☐ ____

☐ ____

28. From what source have you received the least useful information about the world problem of ____________?

☐ ____

28A. Why, compared to the other sources you have mentioned, was ____________ the least useful?

☐ ____

☐ ____

☐ ____

29. From which of these sources have you received the most information about the world problem of ______________?

☐ ____

30. From what source have you received the least information about the world problem of ______________?

☐ ____

31. From what source have you received the most trustworthy information about the world problem of ______________?

☐ ____

32. From what source have you received the least trustworthy information about the world problem of ______________?

☐ ____

If respondent said "don't know" to Question 26: "What should be done to solve the world problem of ________? do not ask him Questions 33 and 34.

33. Which source helped you most to determine the solutions for t the world problem of ______________?

☐ ____

34. Which source helped you the least to determine the solutions to the world problem of ______________?

☐ ____

35. How long have you lived in (Belgrade) (Ljubljana) (Seattle)?

☐ ____

36. Have you ever lived in a village? (omitted in Seattle)

☐ Yes

☐ No

☐ Don't know

37. Have you ever lived in a small town?

☐ Yes
☐ No
☐ Don't know

38. What is your profession?

☐ ______________________________

39. Are you employed at the present time?

☐ Yes
☐ No. Go to Question 40.

39A. What is your present occupation?

☐ ______________________________

40. What was the occupation of your father?

☐ ______________________________

41. What schools have you attended?

☐ ______________________________
☐ ______________________________
☐ ______________________________
☐ ______________________________

If the respondent didn't specify the type of schools he attended, ask for each school he lists: What kind?

41A. What was the highest school you completed?

☐ ______________________________

If the respondent didn't specify the kind of school, ask: What kind?

GIVE THE RESPONDENT THE INCOME CARD

42. Here is a card showing different income groups.
Just give me the number of the group your family is in:

1 ☐	Under $3,000/year	Under 1,000 new dinar a month
2 ☐	$3,000 to $4,999	1,000 to 2,000
3 ☐	$5,000 to $6,999	3,000 to 4,000
4 ☐	$7,000 to $9,999	4,000 to 5,000
5 ☐	$10,000 to $14,999	5,000 to 6,000
6 ☐	$15,000 to $19,999	6,000 to 7,000
7 ☐	$20,000 and over	7,000 to 8,000
8 ☐	Refused	8,000 to 9,000
9 ☐	Don't know	

43. How many members are there in your household?

☐ ______________________

If only one,
go to Question 44.

43A. For the adult members, tell me, one by one, their present occupations and the highest schools they have completed.

Household member	Present occupation	Highest school

44. How old are you?

☐ ______________________

45. What is your marital status?

☐ Single
☐ Married

☐ Divorced

☐ Widowed

46. Sex

☐ Male

☐ Female

Thank you very much for your cooperation. Your answers will help us find out how certain mass media and other sources of information help our people to see and solve important problems. This interview is a part of a larger study whose results will be published by the (University of Washington) (the Yugoslav Institute for Journalism)

48. Have you any remarks on our questionnaire?

☐ ____________________

☐ ____________________

____

____

Thank you once again.

Time at end of interview: ____________

APPENDIX B

INSTRUCTIONS TO INTERVIEWERS

Purposes of our study

We want to learn more about the individual who is encountering social problems that are important to him.

This study is being done crossculturally. It is being done also in (Belgrade) (Ljubljana) (Seattle).

We are developing a distinctive methodology that depends very much upon the skill of the interviewer.

You will note that the questionnaire is open-ended in many places, but it is very precise in its structure. We have very definite expectations for the kinds of answers that we will get to questions.

Interviewer role

You can see that the interviewer has a very special role in this type of interview.

You must be very attentive to what the respondent says.

You must write down everything that the respondent says. You must write it down precisely.

To accommodate this problem of (1) attentiveness versus (2) the need to record all statements we suggest the following procedure:

In answer to open-ended questions:

1. Listen carefully to what the respondent says.
2. After he has finished speaking, write down what he says.
3. As you write, orally repeat what you are writing. The purposes of this are (1) to permit the respondent to correct you or to correct himself and (2) to permit him to give you additional information.

When there is a probe to an open-ended question, you must ask it, even if in your personal judgment the respondent has given you all the information available to him, and you must ask the probe even if the respondent has specifically stated: "That is all." Just smile and ask the probe.

The probes are very important. There is a circle opposite each probe. As you ask the probe, place an X inside the circle. This tells us if you have asked the probe. Otherwise, we will not be certain.

All questions and probes must be asked exactly as they are stated. There must be no variation in phrasing.

If a respondent does not understand the question, or if he asks for some information about the question, do not give it. Instead, simply repeat the question, a second time, more slowly. If the respondent still cannot answer, you should say: "Well, let's go on to the next question."

The respondent may understand the next question and then be able to go back and answer the previous question.

Selecting the household

1. You will be given a sampling area that is a convenient as possible for you, but since we have a random sample there will be some traveling for everyone.

2. We ask that you do at least three interviews a day, but no more than five. This is to prevent excessive fatigue on your part.

3. We ask also that you vary the time of the interviews. Do at least one half of them in the evening, nonworking hours when people are available in their homes.

4. You should in your own interest carefully plan the area in which you conduct your interviews so that you lose as little time as possible in travel. This will be easy at the beginning, but as you complete interviews, the remaining places will become more widely separated.

5. If you do not find the person on your first call, and someone is at home, try to discover when your respondent will be at home. If possible, arrange an appointment. If no one is at home, and if you call back on another day, make it at a different time. If the person was not at home in the afternoon, call back in the evening or in the morning. People generally have a daily routine, whether they have a job or not, and the probability is that they do similar things at similar times.

6. If the person who is on your list is dead, ill, or otherwise unable to complete an interview, go to the next person on your reserve list. Do not interview another person in the same household.

Do not refuse to interview elderly people just because they are old; only if they are incapable. If they are alert and responsive, you should conduct the interview. Do not disqualify old people simply because they are uninformed. We are interested in the relationship between age and community participation, so you would deprive us of information we require.

7. We have worked very carefully to construct this sample. We enumerated the number of people in every opština, sampled in every area, and obtained the names of each person. Each person was then listed on the sheets that will be given to you. This is an enormous amount of work. It is only justified if you make every effort to interview those persons who were selected. Please make at

least two callbacks in an effort to obtain the person who is on your basic list. Use as few persons on your reserve list as is possible.

Keeping your records

When you have completed an interview, write "completed" or "C" opposite the name.

When a person is not home, write "not home" or "NH" opposite his name and the date and time that you called. Do this each time you call. It will be useful information to you and to us as well.

You will notice that there are blank boxes where you will be writing the answers to open-ended questions. Leave these blanks free. We will write numbers in those boxes.

Problem interviews

If you have an uncooperative or hostile respondent, please advise us by telephone as soon after the interview as possible. The number is ________.

If you are asked about the purposes of the interview, you should give only that information contained in the introduction, which should be sufficient. If the respondent wishes more information, give him the telephone number and tell him to ask for ________________.

You will carry with you an official letter of designation as an interviewer. You may show this to anyone on request.

Obtaining the interview

If the respondent ask you how long the interview will take, you may say "approximately 20 minutes, but this depends upon the person".

If there is obvious resistance due to the pressure upon the respondent of some other activity, make another appointment.

If the respondent is reluctant to be interviewed, you may offer the following reasons in an effort to persuade him:

- "It would hurt the project if you did not participate because your views are important."
- "Your name was chosen because of mathematical calculations. If you do not participate, we will have a mathematical error."
- "If people refuse, we cannot finish the work, and the work is very important."
- "Your opinion might not seem important to you, but every piece of the picture is important. When we put it all together we will have a full picture."

Conducting the interview

Be courteous and attentive, but not too friendly. Do not permit the respondent to develop a relationship with you where he seeks your approval in any way.

You may say "yes" as an acknowledgement that the person has said something, but do not say "yes" in such a way that the respondent might think that you are agreeing with what he said.

Isolate the respondent physically. Ask others to excuse you. This is very important in an open-ended interview. If necessary, go outside with the respondent to get him away from a crowded setting. No one should be permitted to listen or to observe, whether wife or husband, daughter or son.

At the conclusion of the interview, say to the respondent: "Let me see if I have missed anything." Then go through the questionnaire to see if there are any missing data. This may also give the respondent a chance to add information.

Concluding the interview

Be certain to write down the time that the interview was concluded. Ask the respondent if he has a telephone so that if there are any problems you can call him. Record the telephone number.

Sample and quotas

Our total sample is ________ selected very carefully on a random basis. We expect to begin interviewing on ______________ and complete the work within 10 days. That means that each interviewer will have to complete his quota within that time.

Training schedule

You should do a practice interview tonight in your home. Please bring it tomorrow for discussion purposes.

Reinterview procedure

We are very interested in interaction between interviewers and respondents and will ourselves telephone and revisit a large number of respondents. If you are interested in the respondent's remarks about interviews you have conducted, we will make this information available to you. Please, however, do not tell the respondent that he may be reinterviewed.

We will now go through the questionnaire item by item to clear up any misunderstandings.

SUPPLEMENTAL INSTRUCTIONS*

Please read carefully. We have examined the practice interviews and a serious error is being made by several of the interviewers:

In Question 5 we ask how the person learned about the local problem. In Question 5A we ask a probe about how the person learned about the local problem. Answers to both the question and the probe must be placed on the green sheet for purposes of comparing the media.

In Question 22 we ask how the person learned about the world problem. In Question 22 we ask a probe.

Answers to both the question and the probe must be put on the yellow sheet for purposes of comparing the media. Do not forget to include information from the probe when you circle the sources of information that the respondent has given you.

Question	Explanation or change
4	If the respondent says " ________ " is the most important problem to me, but the others are far more important to others, you must still ask about the individual's problem.
4A	If the respondent gives a general response, such as "some time ago," please probe by asking "When was that?" or "Can you give me a more definite time?" It is possible that they might give you an "event" such as "when __________ happened".
10-17A 27-34A	If only one source of information was mentioned in response to Question 5 or Question 22, do not ask the media evaluation questions 10-17A for local problems or the media evaluation questions 27-34A for world problems.

---

*These supplemental instructions were given in Belgrade, Ljubljana, and Seattle, as appropriate, upon receipt of the first two to four completed interviews.

Question	Explanation or change
9A 26A	If respondent asks what you mean by "other solutions," you may reply: "any other solution" or "anyone else's solution,"
9B 26B	Take our Questions 9B and 26B only.
16A 17A 33A 34A	The respondent must define for himself what "useful" means to him. Do not give him any information. Useful can mean many things and we are interested in learning what they are.
39A	Get the specific occupation. If respondent says: "worker," probe and ask, "What kind of work?" If respondent says "retired," probe and ask him what his occupation was before he retired.
41	If respondent has a certificate that states that he has passed examinations equivalent to a certain year of school, write this down. However, also find out how many actual, full-time years of school the respondent completed.
41 43A	If the respondent begins by telling you about a higher school, write this down. Do not go back and ask him or members of his family.
42	If a student lives alone, put down only his private income. If a student lives with his family, put down the total family income. The same rules apply to those who are divorced.

BIBLIOGRAPHY

Bacević, Ljiljana. 1965a. "Efficiency of Specific Mass Media." In Mass Media in Yugoslavia: Readers, Listeners, Watchers. Belgrade: Yugoslav Institute of Journalism and Institute of Social Sciences.

________. 1965b. "Exposure to Influence of Specific Media." In Mass Media in Yugoslavia: Readers, Listeners, Watchers. Belgrade: Yugoslav Institute of Journalism and Institute of Social Sciences.

________. 1965c. "Index of Utilisation of Mass Media." In Mass Media in Yugoslavia: Readers, Listeners, Watchers. Belgrade: Yugoslav Institute of Journalism and Institute of Social Sciences.

Barton, Allen H.; Bogdan Denitch; and Charles Kadushin, eds. 1973. Opinion-Making Elites in Yugoslavia. New York: Praeger Publishers.

Begović, Bruno. 1967. "Inquiry of Yugoslav Periodicals in 1966." Novinarstvo (Journalism) no. 4. Belgrade: Yugoslav Institute of Journalism.

Blejeć, Marijan. 1970. Nacrti in Analiza Vzorcev za Ankete Slovensko Javno Mnenje. Fakulteta za Sociologijo, Politica ede in Novinarstvo. Ljubljana: University of Ljubljana, May 1970.

Bosnić, Slobodan. 1969. "Demographic, Economic, and Educational Features of Yugoslav Population Which Affect the Distribution of Mass Media." In Factors and Ways of Expansion of Mass Media in Yugoslavia, Belgrade: Yugoslav Institute of Journalism.

Bush, Chilton R. 1966. News Research for Better Newspapers, Vol. I. New York: American Newspaper Publishers Association.

________. 1967. News Research for Better Newspapers, Vol. II. New York: American Newspapers Publishers Association.

Carter, Richard F., and Bradley S. Greenberg, 1965. "Newspapers and Television: Which Do You Believe?" Journalism Quarterly, 42: 29-34.

Clark, Dan E. II & Associates. 1965. Miami Herald Market and Audience Study. Miami, Fla.

Danojlić, Jelena. 1965a. "Motivation for Use of Mass Media." In Mass Media in Yugoslavia: Readers, Listeners, Watchers. Belgrade: Yugoslav Institute of Journalism and Institute of Social Sciences.

________. 1965b. "Preference of Specific Media." In Mass Media in Yugoslavia: Readers, Listeners, Watchers. Belgrade: Yugoslav Institute of Journalism and Institute of Social Sciences.

________. 1965c. "Public Criticism of Mass Media." In Mass Media in Yugoslavia: Readers, Listeners, Watchers. Belgrade: Yugoslav Institute of Journalism and Institute of Social Sciences.

________. 1965d. "Quality of Interaction of Particular Media and Its Users." In Mass Media in Yugoslavia: Readers, Listeners, Watchers. Belgrade: Yugoslav Institute of Journalism and Institute of Social Sciences.

________. 1968. "TV and Cultural Activities." Novinarstvo, nos. 1-2. Belgrade: Yugoslav Institute of Journalism.

________. 1969a. "Some Views of the Exposure to Press and of Motivation of Readers." In Factors and Ways of Expansion of Mass Media in Yugoslavia. Belgrade: Yugoslav Institute of Journalism.

________. 1969b. "Study of Readers and Nonreaders of Press." In Factors and Ways of Expansion of Mass Media in Yugoslavia. Belgrade: Yugoslav Institute of Journalism.

Dimković, Borislav J. 1967. "Informedness of Workers About the Operation and Life of Their Enterprise." Novinarstvo, no. 1. Belgrade: Yugoslav Institute of Journalism.

Djordjević, Miroslav. 1970. "New Year's Eve Shows of Radio and TV as Determinants of Audience Behavior." In Utilisation of Public Information. Belgrade: Yugoslav Institute of Journalism.

Dzinić, Dr. Firdus. 1970. "Expansion of Political-Informative Effect of Radio, TV and Press in Yugoslavia." In Utilisation of Public Information. Belgrade: Yugoslav Institute of Journalism.

Edelstein, Alex. 1966. Perspectives in Mass Communication. Copenhagen: Einar Harck.

________. 1969a. "Communication and International Conflict." In France Vreg., ed., Mass Media and International Understanding. Ljubljana; Higher School for Political Science and Journalism.

________. 1969b. "The Public Opinion Polls as a Source of Distortion in the International Flow of News." Paper prepared for XVII International Symposium, International Centre for Higher Education, Strasbourg, France, December 8-13, 1969.

________. 1974. "Decision-Making and Mass Communication: A Conceptual and Methodological Approach to Public Opinion." In Peter Clarke and F. Gerald Kline, eds., New Models for Communication Research. Beverly Hills, Calif.: SAGE Publications (in press).

________, with Neil Hollander. 1968. "Communication and International Conflict: A Preliminary Appraisal." Paper presented at International Symposium on International Understanding through Communication, Ljubljana, September 2-5, 1968.

________. 1970. "Attribute Structure, Education and Communication with Respect to Vietnam." Paper prepared for International Communication Division, Association for Education in Journalism, Washington, D. C., August 1970.

Greenberg, Bradley S., and Brenda Dervin, 1967. Communication Among The Urban Poor, Report #1, Michigan State University, East Lansing, Mich.

Guzina, Milica, and Ivan Stajnberger. 1970. "General Characteristics and Attitudes of Workers Toward Factory Press." In Utilisation of Public Information. Belgrade: Yugoslav Institute of Journalism.

Institut Za Sociologijo in Filozofijo pri Univerzi v Ljubljani. (Institute for Sociology and Philosophy) Radio 1967: Raziskava O. Mnenjih in Stalisch Poslusalcev Do Sporeda. (Study of the Regular Listening Audiences) Ljubljana: Radio Ljubljana. October 1967.

Kline, F. Gerald, and Phillip J. Tichenor. 1972. Current Perspectives in Mass Communication Research, 1972. Beverly Hills, Calif.:

Sage Publications, Annual Reviews of Communications Research, Vol. I.

Kroflić, M.; S. Obranović; and A. Stupan. 1968. Televizija 67. Ljubljana: Institut za Sociologijo in Filozofijo Pri Univerzi v Ljubljana, August 1968.

Leandrov, Igor. 1967a. "Communication Channels and Information Groups." Press, Radio and TV in Self-Management System. Proceedings of symposium held under the same title in Belgrade, January 11-12, 1967. Belgrade: Yugoslav Institute of Journalism.

________. 1967b. "Channels of Communication, Elements of the Process of Information, Information Groups." Novinarstvo, nos. 2-3. Belgrade: Yugoslav Institute of Journalism.

Letica, Zvonko. 1966. "TV News Zagreb," a review. Novinarstvo, no. 4. Belgrade: Yugoslav Institute of Journalism.

Lyle, Jack and Richard A. Stone, 1971. Election Coverage and Audience Reactions, Santa Monica, Calif., Mimeo, 27 pp., University of California at Los Angeles.

Majstorović, Stevan. 1970. The Cultural Policy of Yugoslavia. Belgrade: UNESCO.

Marjanović, Stevan. 1968. "Graphic Basis of Yugoslav Periodicals." Novinarstvo, nos. 1-2. Belgrade: Yugoslav Institute of Journalism.

Mishra, Vishwa Mohan. 1972. Communication and Modernization in Urban Slums. New York: Asia Publishing House.

Misović, Milos. 1970. "Popularity and Trustworthiness." In Utilisation of Public Information. Proceedings of symposium held in Belgrade, December 22-23, 1969. Belgrade: Yugoslav Institute of Journalism.

Nastić, Slavko. 1967. "Motivation for Asking Information as One of the Premises of Utilisation of the Rights to be Informed." In Press, Radio and TV in Self-Management. Belgrade: Yugoslav Institute of Journalism.

News and Editorial Content and Readership of the Daily Newspaper. 1966. New York: American Newspaper Publishers Association.

News Research Bulletins, 1967-73. In seriatum. New York: American Newspaper Publishers Association.

Novinarstvo. 1967. Nos. 1-4. Belgrade: Yugoslav Institute of Journalism.

________, 1968. Nos. 1-4. Belgrade: Yugoslav Institute of Journalism.

________, 1969. Nos. 1-2. Belgrade: Yugoslav Institute of Journalism.

Obradović, Stane, and Ana Stupan. 1968. "Public Attitudes about Central Informative TV Programs." Novinarstvo, nos. 3-4. Belgrade: Yugoslav Institute of Journalism.

Opinion Research Corp., 1975. News and Editorial Content and Readership of the Daily Newspaper, News Research Bulletin 5, American Newspaper Publishers Association.

Ostojić, Neda. 1970. "Effect of Education on Preference of Radio and TV Broadcasts." In Utilisation of Public Information. Belgrade: Yugoslav Institute of Journalism.

Plavsić, Prvoslav. 1969. "Frequency of Listening to Radio." In Factors and Ways of Expansion of Mass Media in Yugoslavia. Belgrade: Yugoslav Institute of Journalism.

________, and Dr. Dragan Krstić. 1969. "Study of the Users of Mass Media in Yugoslavia." In Factors and Ways of Expansion of Mass Media in Yugoslavia. Belgrade: Yugoslav Institute of Journalism.

Pustisek, Dr. Ivko. 1970. "Financial State of Radio and TV in Yugoslavia." In Utilisation of Public Information. Belgrade: Yugoslav Institute of Journalism.

Robinson, Gertrude J. 1973. "The Mass Media and Nation-Building: Testing a Hypothesis in Multi-National Yugoslavia." Paper prepared for International Communications Association, Montreal, Canada, April 25-28, 1973.

Roper, Burns, 1972. What People Think of Television And Other Mass Media, 1959-1972, A Report by the Roper Organization, Inc.

Schramm, Wilbur. 1954. The Process and Effects of Mass Communication. Urbana, Ill.: University of Illinois Press.

Slovensko, Javno Mnenje, 69. 1970. (Slovenian Public Opinion, 1969) Visoka Sola za Sociologio Politicne vede in Novinarstvo, April 1970. (Higher School for Sociology, Political Science, and Journalism)

Sokolović, Srdjan. 1969. "Attitude of Audience Towards the Movie News." In Factors and Ways of Expansion of Mass Media in Yugoslavia. Belgrade: Yugoslav Institute of Journalism.

Stajnberger, Ivan. 1970. "Some Conditions of Informedness of Workers." In Utilisation of Public Information. Belgrade: Yugoslav Institute of Journalism.

Stoković, Zivorad. 1966. "Radio and TV Subscribers in Yugoslavia in 1966." Novinarstvo, no. 4. Belgrade: Yugoslav Institute of Journalism.

Todorović, Dr. Aleksander. 1970. "Role of Mass Media in Development of Movie Preference Among Youth." In Utilisation of Public Information. Belgrade: Yugoslav Institute of Journalism.

Vreg, France. Slovensko Javno Mnenje. 1969. (Slovenian Public Opinion) Ljubljana: Center Za Raziskovanje Javnega Mnenja in Mnozicnih Komunikacij. (Center for the Study of Public Opinion and Mass Communication)

Westley, Bruce H., and Werner Severin, 1964a. "Some Correlates of Mass Media Credibility," Journalism Quarterly, 41: 325-35.

________, 1964b. "A Profile of the Daily Newspaper Non-Reader," Journalism Quarterly, 41: 45-51.

Wright, Charles. 1959. Mass Communication: A Sociological Perspective. New York: Random House.

ABOUT THE AUTHOR

ALEX S. EDELSTEIN is Professor and Director of the School of Communications at the University of Washington. At one time a journalist, Dr. Edelstein also has a background in mass communication and international communication research.

Dr. Edelstein is the author of Perspectives in Mass Communication, published in 1966. He is on the editorial board of several journals in communication and publishes both here and abroad. He has been an officer in scholarly organizations in the United States and overseas. He was a Fulbright lecturer to Denmark in 1963-64 and has lectured in Eastern and Western Europe, Scandinavia, Latin America, and Japan.

Dr. Edelstein holds an M.A. from Stanford University and a Ph.D. from the University of Minnesota.

RELATED TITLES
Published by
Praeger Special Studies

ASPEN NOTEBOOK ON GOVERNMENT AND THE MEDIA Sponsored by the Aspen Institute Program on Communications and Society
edited by William L. Rivers and Michael J. Nyhan

MASS COMMUNICATION AND CONFLICT RESOLUTION: The Role of the Information Media in the Advancement of International Understanding
W. Phillips Davison

MASS COMMUNICATION RESEARCH: Major Issues and Future Directions
edited by W. Phillips Davison and Frederick T. C. Yu

OPINION-MAKING ELITES IN YUGOSLAVIA
edited by Allen H. Barton, Bogdan Denitch, and Charles Kadushin